GARDEN *Style*

Ideas & Projects
for Your World

JERRI FARRIS AND TIM HIMSEL

CREATIVE
PUBLISHING
international

MINNETONKA, MINNESOTA

www.creativepub.com

PUYALLUP PUBLIC LIBRARY

747
Parris

CONTENTS

PROJECTS

$\mathscr{P}$REFACE

My interest in garden-style decorating grew out of my love for gardening, but neither began to bloom until later in my life. Growing up in the Ozark Mountains of southern Missouri, gardening was not my favorite activity. Afternoons spent in the blazing heat and humidity, dodging snakes and weeding my mom's vegetable patch or flower beds were a form of slow torture for me. My lack of enthusiasm continued into adulthood.

Then came the day when I abruptly found myself single again, caring for two children and a suburban home alone. I was two steps beyond terrified. In an attempt to distract myself, I tore out a landscaping bed in the front yard and planted my first perennials. At the time it was a way to keep busy, to keep myself from going crazy. It became something entirely different.

The next spring, when shoots peeked out into the watery Minnesota sunshine, I was reborn right along with the garden. Amazed that I'd managed to establish something beautiful in the midst of such chaos, I watered and weeded and puttered. Most of all, I began to dream again. Of building new perennial beds, of building a new life. Gardening took root in my soul.

When winter arrived, my heart was still in the garden. With nothing constructive to do outdoors, I began to imagine ways to bring the feeling of the garden into my house and my interest in garden style emerged. The picket fence shelf shown on page 79 is the first thing I ever built. I laboriously made the few necessary cuts with a handsaw because I was afraid to use power tools. Before spring, I had even braved a circular saw in order to build a garden-style bench.

Now, my home is a combination of traditional furniture, flea market finds, and antiques—much of it related in one way or another to gardening or to family stories or to both. On even the grayest November afternoon or the bitterest of January mornings, this eclectic mix warms and comforts me.

Tim Himsel and Jerri Farris

The voice you hear throughout these pages is mine. Much of what you see is the work of my friend and creative partner, the incomparable Tim Himsel. A graphics artist and creative director, Tim designed the look of the book as well as many of the projects. His talent, imagination, and creativity are reflected on every single page.

Tim has a knack for turning our wildest ideas into achievable realities. As you'll find in some of the stories that follow, he grew up on a farm in southern Wisconsin. I think his mechanical abilities were honed on the farm, where machinery and equipment was repaired and adapted year after year. His artistic abilities, on the other hand, are pure gift. On both counts, I'm grateful for the opportunity to work with Tim and to learn from him.

Tim and I have been privileged to work with a talented, generous group of people, and together we created something no one of us could have done alone. We'd especially like to thank Terrie Myers, Paul Gorton, Dan Widerski, Julie Caruso, John Rajtar, and Tate Carlson, who helped design, build, and photograph the projects.

Jerri Farris

$\mathscr{I}$NTRODUCTION

What exactly is garden style?

Garden style embodies the spirit of the garden and the gardener. It incorporates colors, textures, materials, and themes that radiate the beauty and simplicity of nature. Garden-style homes, like gardens, are entirely individual—they can be as highly structured as a formal garden or as wonderfully random as a country meadow. Although no two are alike, they have common elements.

Just as gardens are built over time, so are garden-style rooms. They exude a sense of emergence, of having been developed thoughtfully and tended carefully. And as with heirloom plants and seeds, the furnishings and accessories are cherished for their memories and their meanings.

Gardens and garden-style rooms are tailored to meet the needs of the people who use them. Every element is right for its place and all the pieces work together to support the purpose of the room and to refresh the souls of those who live there.

For dedicated gardeners, garden-style decorating is a natural extension, a way to live in the garden, year-round. In most climates, there is at least one season that's inhospitable to outdoor activities. Whether our gardens shiver in frigid windchills or wither in scorching heat, there's bound to be a time when they lie fallow. Our interest, however, doesn't dwindle during that time; we plan and dream and wait, somewhat impatiently.

For others, the connection to the garden is more a matter of spirit than of practice. High-rise dwellers or other urban folks may lack the space for a garden; parents of young children or people with extremely busy careers may lack the time; people with serious health problems or physical limitations may lack the capacity. But even for these folks, the spirit of the garden beckons.

Whatever the reasons may be, more and more people are turning to the pleasures of creating indoor settings that echo the magical shapes, colors, textures, scents, and traditions of a garden. Garden style is a strong and growing trend. Catalogs and retail stores are filled with furnishings and accessories centered on garden themes and there are hundreds of web sites dedicated to the same.

Gardens are filled with personality, memories and dreams. Creating a garden-style home is as simple as finding ways to bring the spirit of a garden into your home. But how do you do that? Where do you begin?

In his wonderful book, *The Principles of Gardening*, Hugh Johnson tells us, "Observation is where style starts." Before you begin adding garden-style furnishings or accessories to your home, invest some time observing a garden and your responses to it. Sit quietly in its midst or, if that's not practical, imagine yourself there. Think about what appeals to you most, what draws you back again and again. Ask yourself what areas you find most inviting and what it is that intrigues you. Is it color? Fragrance? Sound? Memories?

Once you've defined the aspects that you love most, create ways to bring them indoors. If it's fragrance that makes your heart sing, add aromatic houseplants or floral sachets or pomander balls to your rooms. If a garden fountain calls to your spirit, add a tabletop version in a quiet place, away from the flow of traffic. If shaped shrubs are among your favorites, try growing a topiary or a bonsai. In short, reach beyond floral fabrics and themed furnishings to your own heart and soul—that's where garden style truly begins.

When I first tried this exercise, I found myself sitting beside a Peace rose climber that scrambles over a copper trellis. My folks kept a rose garden when I was growing up, and Mom's favorite of all the roses was the Peace. My dad dusted and coddled that rose bush, and my mom happily watched every stage of its blooming. I had planted a Peace rose in my own garden to honor those memories, and I now wanted somehow to bring them into my home. The most appealing thing about a Peace is its coloration—soft yellow giving way to pink. And so, I painted my foyer and much of the first floor in a lovely creamy yellow and then added pink accents here and there. The result is a beautiful, warm, sunny space where I feel right at home.

My garden speaks to me. Literally, through words carved into stones and a handful of small brass plaques placed in flower beds. I transplanted that idea into the house, too, and began writing on my walls. Now Christopher Robin calls out from above the family room doorway, reminding my children and me that we are braver than we believe and stronger than we know. From above a mirror, Proust points out that the real voyage of discovery consists not of seeking new landscapes, but of having new eyes. My bathroom walls sport quotes attributed to everyone from Goethe to Janis Joplin. Unusual, but it suits me perfectly, and that's what matters.

Start by dreaming and imagining—over time your home can come to reflect not only a garden, but your self.

The most basic principle of planning an outdoor garden is to start with plants that are indigenous to the area. In much the same way, garden style starts with what you already have in your home. Before you go shopping, evaluate the materials you already own.

If you have houseplants, mass them to produce the effect of a border. If you have linens or accessories that support the theme, bring them out of storage and find places for them. Just as wood always looks at home in a garden, simple wood furniture is effective in a garden room. Brick and stone almost always find places in garden rooms.

Even pieces that have no direct connection to gardening can become part of the strategy. Mirrors, for example, can play an important part. Placed to reflect plants or floral arrangements, or even to reflect and multiply the available light, they can contribute to the ambience you're creating.

Before you do anything else, put your imagination to work.

Combining vintage and new furnishings and accessories creates the relaxed, eclectic charm that's a fundamental part of garden style. Worn finishes, heirloom linens, odd shapes, and interesting textures are at home here.

With that kind of background, an entire room can be refreshed by a temporary infusion of color or a seasonal theme. Here's one great idea—collect several dozen small, inexpensive, clear glass vases. When you want to make a big splash, fill each vase with one or two stems of simple flowers. Arrange groups of vases to produce the illusion of a room-sized bouquet.

Color works to help blur the boundaries between the house and garden. It can be used to reinforce the theme and suggest a mood; it can increase or decrease the feeling of space by the way it reflects or absorbs light. Understanding color and using it well is especially important in garden-style decorating.

If you want to study color theory, start at a bookstore or library—you'll find many fine books on the subject. I'm not an expert by any means, and we don't have room here to go into great detail, but there are a few fundamentals that will carry you a long way.

It's helpful to start with the understanding that color is reflected light changed by the surface off of which it's reflected. Once you get that concept down, it's easy to recognize how much color is affected by light. Strong light has to be balanced with vibrant color—pastel or pale colors simply wash away. In dim light, strong colors seem garish, but pastels appear to glow.

Climate and weather conditions have a surprising impact on decorating customs. In locales where the natural light is brilliant, it is traditional to use intense colors. In temperate zones, the traditional colors tend toward pastels and pale tones. This hasn't happened by accident but in response to the basic laws of nature, and it applies both indoors and out.

In garden-style rooms, many colors mingle with shades of green to reproduce the palette of a garden. These combinations are often set against white backgrounds, because white makes them appear richer. White light, as Sir Isaac Newton discovered, contains all other colors. That explains its ability to change subtly, depending on the colors that surround it. As you're working with color, remember that you rarely see only one color at a time. Each is affected by its interaction with the surrounding colors and by the context of the setting.

Garden rooms often rely on a palette of neutrals livened up by occasional colorful accents. Neutral schemes can be very successful, especially if the backdrops, furnishings, and accessories include a broad range of textures, such as wood, stone, tile, metal, fabric, and fiber.

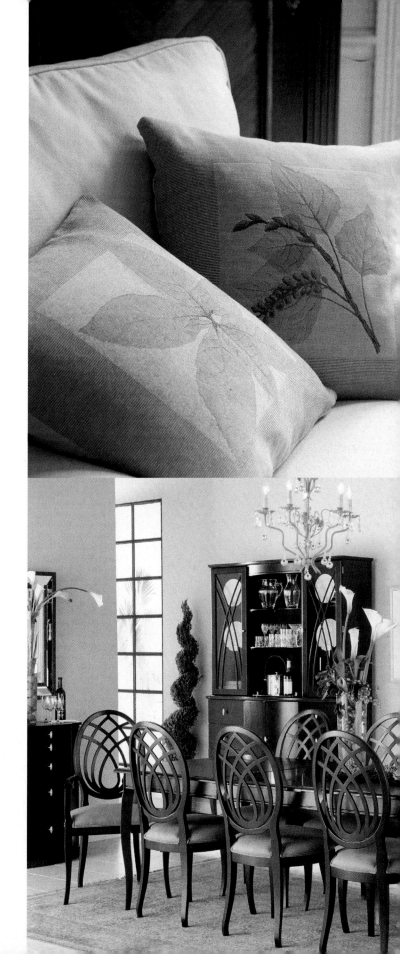

$\mathcal{B}$ACKDROPS

Trees are the tallest natural element in most landscapes. Along with the contours of the land itself, they provide a sense of scale and structure. These are the backdrops that define and describe a garden. In the very same way, walls, windows, doors, and floors provide the scale and the boundaries for a room. However, these backdrops can be much more than functional—they can act as decorative features in their own right.

Walls typically are the largest backdrop in the room, and with the right treatment, they can set the stage for all that follows. You can use special paint effects to imitate the texture of natural materials, alter perceptions of the room's light through colorwashing, or literally draw the outdoors in with trompe l'oeil.

The next most prominent backdrops are windows and doors. Imaginative window treatments can support the theme and emphasize the views. You can't overestimate the importance of light to a garden room, and window treatments can be used to enhance the quality of the available light. Give some thought to each room's orientation and the patterns of sunlight that surround the house. It may be necessary to use window treatments that filter strong afternoon sun or to leave the windows as open as possible to maximize the ambient light in a shady corner.

Though often overlooked, floors present another opportunity to reinforce the garden theme. Traditional hardscape materials, such as stone, brick, and wood are good flooring choices for garden rooms. Area rugs, floor cloths, and special paint effects also can be used to introduce color, texture, or character that reflects the ambience of a garden.

WINDOW TREATMENTS

In the plant world, sunlight equals energy, and it's much the same for people. Light, lively rooms are the essence of garden style, so windows and window treatments are especially important. In the sitting room at left, light streams into the room through the broad expanse of windows. With its colorful fabric and stylized shape, the valance dresses the windows without interfering with the view or limiting the available light. Depending on the orientation of your room and privacy considerations, it may be necessary to filter the light in some way, but window treatments for garden-style rooms should enhance, rather than obscure, the windows.

Window treatments also offer an opportunity to reinforce the theme through fabrics, texture, and style. In the example shown above, a small vase acts as a tie-back. Silk or dried flowers are practical, but fresh ones make a lovely statement for special occasions.

Many window dressings typically found outside also make wonderful interior accessories. Window boxes, shutters, and even trellises, such as the ones shown at right, can be moved indoors to provide unexpected touches that produce a playful atmosphere. On pages 28 and 29 we show you how to use shutters and a window box to create a unique backdrop for a garden room. Another great idea would be to bring a trellis indoors—you could even train ivy to grow over it. Be sure to anchor the trellis to the wall with sturdy hardware so that it can't be knocked over.

It would be impossible to be in a bad mood in the bright, cheerful bathroom shown above. Latticework shutters establish the theme, which is emphasized by the decorative painting on the vanity as well as the other accessories. The neutral tones used throughout the room provide a perfect background for live plants and dried flowers.

FAIRY TALES

Gardening is an act of faith. We plant seeds and tend them in the belief that the plants we expect will emerge. We dig up rose bushes in the spring, trusting that those bare sticks will produce blossoms. Most of us find a certain amount of peace while digging in the earth.

The spiritual aspects of gardening have not been lost on the manufacturers of garden accessories. Pixies, fairies, angels, leaf folk—you'll find them all represented among the ornaments displayed in any garden center or shop. If you've become fond of those leafy little faces, you might enjoy bringing them indoors as part of this interesting, easy-to-make cornice board.

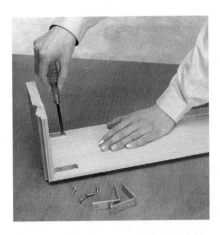

1 Measure the window and locate the wall studs in the area. Keeping in mind that the weight must be supported by studs, determine the length of the cornice board. Cut the molding to fit, mitering the ends at 45° angles. Glue and locknail the joints. Using ½" (12 mm) wood screws and angle irons, reinforce the joints from the back. Paint or stain the molding as desired.

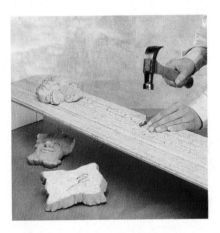

2 Calculate even spacing, drill pilot holes, and attach picture hangers to the molding. Hang a garden plaque from each picture hanger.

3 Drill pilot holes, then use screws to attach angle irons to the wall on each side of the window. Be sure you hit the studs with each screw, or use hollow wall anchors rated for the anticipated load. Hold the cornice in place, drill pilot holes, and attach the installed angle irons to the inside back edges of the cornice.

MATERIALS:

6" (15 CM) MOLDING • ANGLE IRONS (8)
• 2" (5 CM) WOOD SCREWS (6) • ½" (12 MM) WOOD SCREWS (6)
• PAINT • PICTURE HANGERS (3) • GARDEN PLAQUES

OUTSIDE IN

There's something so welcoming about plants and flowers peeking out of a window box. By transplanting window boxes and shutters indoors, you can infuse a room with that welcoming spirit. If you select plants that are appropriate for the light they'll receive, they should thrive as they contribute a dash of style to the room.

Note: Even if you use lightweight potting soil, the window box will be heavy when it's planted. Be sure to use sturdy brackets secured to wall studs or supported by hardware designed for the estimated weight of the finished box.

1 Locate studs in the walls and plan the placement of the brackets. If the window is more than 36" (90 cm) wide, use three equally spaced brackets. Install the brackets according to the manufacturer's instructions. Fill the window box with potting soil and add plants. If desired, you can paint the shutters to match or complement the room.

2 Attach swivel hangers to the shutters and picture hangers to the wall, positioning them so the shutters will be centered against the window. Hang the shutters and make sure they're level.

MATERIALS:

WINDOW BOX • BRACKETS (AS SUPPLIED BY MANUFACTURER) • POTTING SOIL
• PLANTS • SWIVEL HANGERS (4) • PICTURE HANGERS (4) • SHUTTERS (2)

FRAMING THE VIEW

To draw the outdoors into a room, think of the windows as art to be framed—you might be surprised at how much more compelling a view becomes when it's surrounded by a unique window treatment like this one made from antique doorknobs.

Note: for windows wider than 40" (1 m), support the rod with three doorknobs.

1 *Loosen the setscrew and remove the stem from each knob. Use two-part epoxy to glue a knob into each escutcheon.*

2 *Locate the studs near the outside edges of the window. Hold each escutcheon in position, mark and drill pilot holes, and use 2" (5 cm) brass screws to hang it. If there are no studs in suitable locations, use wall anchors to support the weight.*

3 *Cut two pieces of silk cord, each about 30" (75 cm) long. Tie a knot 2" (5 cm) above the bottom of each cord; fray the cord below the knot. String beads onto the cord, stacking them to about 4½" (11 cm). Make loops in the cord and hold them in place with several twists of 16-gauge (1.5 mm) copper wire. Stack another inch or two (2.5 to 5 cm) of beads, and knot the cord again. Cut a piece of copper pipe about 16" (40 cm) longer than the window is wide. Glue an end cap to each end of the pipe, then set it on top of the door-knobs. Arrange your fabric or drapes over the pipe and allow it to hang down the sides of the window. Tie the beaded cord to the pipe, between the doorknob and the window trim. Add a brass finial to the endcap, if desired.*

MATERIALS:

ANTIQUE DOORKNOBS AND ESCUTCHEONS
• TWO-PART EPOXY • 2" (5 CM) BRASS SCREWS (4)
• 16-GAUGE (1.5 MM) COPPER WIRE • ½" (12 MM) RIGID COPPER PIPE
• ½" (12 MM) END CAPS (2) • BRASS FINIALS (OPTIONAL)
• 2 YARDS (1.8 M) OF SATIN DRAPERY CORD • BEADS

INGENUITY

Necessity drove me to put my own ingenuity to work on a backdrop—a retaining wall—long before I planted my first perennial. Every time it rained, mud from a badly designed planting area flowed across my front sidewalk. Something had to be done, but I wasn't sure what to do or how to do it. Of course, I headed straight to the bookstore. A book on landscaping soon convinced me that a retaining wall would solve the problem.

The first challenge was finding a way to build the wall without spending a fortune. A landscaping contractor had discarded a fair amount of stone in the marsh behind my house, and I made up my mind to salvage that stone for the wall. Hauling it from the marsh was hot and heavy work, but as I struggled over and over to push heavy wheelbarrow loads up the hill, I felt I was reclaiming more than just the stone.

Building the wall itself turned out to be a satisfying project—much like putting together a life-sized jigsaw puzzle. As it came together, I began to believe in myself and my ability to solve this and other problems facing my children and me.

The first time it rained after the wall was finished, I watched anxiously. It worked! The wall held back the mud. My children and I went out and danced in the clean puddles on our beautiful, mud-free sidewalk, splashing each other and laughing glee-fully. That night I slept better than I had for many months.

When combined with ingenuity, even simple materials bring the magical atmosphere of a garden into your home. The setting shown above incorporates wide molding, a mosaic of floral china, vintage fabric, and a salvaged window sash. These materials aren't expensive or extravagant, but the way they're used creates a whimsical scene that's worth far more than the effort required to produce it.

In the bedroom at right, an oval mirror, a striped awning, and a wrought-iron window box take their places in a trompe l'oeil scene that brightens a dark corner through the ingenious use of simple materials.

As you plan backdrops for your garden rooms, take stock of the materials you have on hand and imagine how they can solve your decorating challenges.

TILED HIGH

From some class in my youth (definitely not math), I remember hearing that the whole is sometimes greater than the sum of the parts. This project is a perfect example of that principle. A piece of cementboard, a few pieces of tile, a couple of trim boards, and a simple layout trick taken from Tim's 8th-grade mechanical drawing textbook add up to an architectural-looking pediment that adds height and interest to a window.

1 Measure the window and cut a square of cementboard to match its width. Draw diagonal lines from corner to corner, forming an X across the square. Set a compass to the distance between one corner and the center of the X. With the point of the compass at each corner in turn, draw a series of arcs that intersect the sides of the square. Connect those points to make an octagon shape. Draw a center line dividing the square into two equal parts. Score and cut the cementboard at the center line; score and cut extra corner triangles to form the shape of the pediment.

continued on page 36

MATERIALS:

CEMENTBOARD • TRIM BOARDS
• PAINT OR STAIN • CERAMIC TILE
• THIN SET MORTAR • GLASS STONES
• HOT GLUE • GROUT
• 2" (5 CM) DRYWALL SCREWS

2 Measure each side of the cementboard and cut trim boards to match, mitering the corners. Paint or stain the pieces and set them aside.

3 Lay out the border tile and mark them for cutting. Use a wet saw or tile cutter to cut the tile to fit. Set the tile in place and draw placement lines on the cementboard. Follow the pattern and mark the design onto the cementboard, or create your own design to complement the tile you've selected. Spread thin-set mortar on the cementboard and set the tile. To set the tile, wrap a short piece of 2 × 4 (5 × 10 cm) in scrap carpeting or a towel. Lay this block over the tile and tap it lightly with a rubber mallet. Let the mortar dry, according to manufacturer's instructions. Use hot glue to attach decorative glass stones to the marked design, then let the glue set.

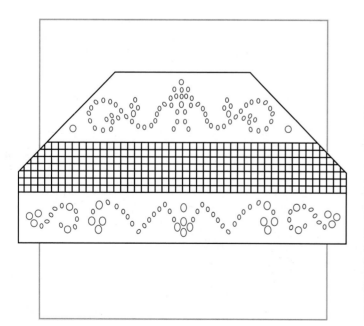

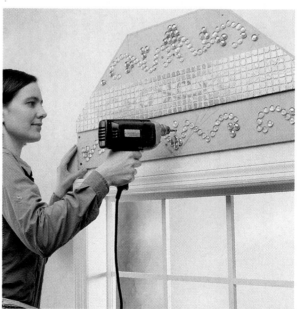

◄4► Locate the studs in the wall above the window. Hold the cementboard in position and mark the stud locations onto it. Drill two or three pilot holes along each marked location, then screw the pediment into position on the wall, using 2" (5 cm) drywall screws.

◄5► Mix latex fortifier into sanded grout. Apply the grout to the pediment, using a sponge to fill the areas surrounding the glass stones, and a grout float to fill the joints between the border tile. Wipe away excess grout with a damp sponge. Let the grout dry for an hour, then polish away the powdery haze with a dry cloth.

◄6► Carefully position the trim pieces at the edges of the cementboard and secure them with construction adhesive. Tape the trim boards in place until the construction adhesive dries completely.

SIMPLY CHARMING

Tim says he learned to draw in self defense. In church, his brother would draw a shape on a tithing envelope and challenge Tim to add lines to make it 3-D. According to Tim, the minister could have wallpapered his study with the envelopes they covered with elaborate drawings.

Few of us have Tim's artistic abilities, but with a little ingenuity we can achieve the effect shown here. Repeating a garden motif from a fabric in the room, such as the draperies or upholstery, creates an elegant, custom-designed look.

1 *Trace the design, then use a photo copier to enlarge or reduce the drawing to produce a pattern.*

2 *Put a piece of graphite paper behind the pattern, and trace the design onto the wall. Use a dull pencil or a stylus, and be careful not to smudge or tear the paper as you work.*

3 *Following the colors and shading of the fabric pattern you're reproducing, paint the design.*

MATERIALS:

TRACING PAPER • GRAPHITE PAPER
• DULL PENCIL OR STYLUS • ACRYLIC PAINT

$\mathcal{F}$URNISHINGS

Furnishings form the foundation of a room in much the same way that shrubs and perennials form the foundation of a garden. Selecting new pieces is something like adding new plantings—each must be appropriate for the conditions and serve some purpose. Ask yourself who uses the room and how, and then select pieces that work well under those conditions. Think of each room as a composition you're creating, and try to balance the shapes, sizes, colors, and textures of its furnishings.

Since few of us can start from scratch when we redecorate, it makes sense to start with the pieces that are already in place, and consider what needs to be eliminated or added. The kind of furnishings that fairly shout "Do Not Touch" have no place in garden-style rooms. The best furnishings for these rooms are informal, gracious pieces that welcome you and invite you to come in and relax. They encourage you to touch and feel and connect with others and with yourself.

To be comfortable, a room needs plenty of resting places—sofas, chairs, beds, benches—where you can think, read, or talk with family and friends. Tables or desks where you can eat, work, or keep lamps and accessories are essential, too.

Every room also needs both open and enclosed storage. For example, I like to keep quilts and other linens in the open (but out of direct sunlight) because they add color and texture. I also need lots of bookshelves and display pieces, because every room in my home contains plants, books, family photographs, and other reminders of the people I love. On the other hand, we all need pieces with doors that can be closed over the clutter that's perpetually waiting for attention.

The HOME
TABLE SETTINGS

AMERICA'S HISTORIC PLACES

FURNITURE

Decorating with Antiques

UNITY

To achieve a sense of unity within your garden room, select colors, materials, and styles that provide a consistent theme. In the breakfast room above, the casual style and subtle color of the hutch are complemented by the fanciful shapes and cheerful colors of the teapot collection it holds.

In the sitting room at left, teak, wicker, and weathered furnishings set a tone that's reinforced by the mixture of new and vintage pieces, as well as the plants and flowers.

NATURAL TEXTURES

Natural materials and textures are particularly at home in garden-style rooms. Simple twig furniture, such as the plant stand shown above and the chair shown on page 73, is surprisingly easy to build. And, since most of the materials are free, it's remarkably inexpensive.

The textures and colors of the chair topiary shown at right beautifully support a garden theme, and can be pulled together with a minimum of fuss and expense. Start with an inexpensive chair—any size, shape or condition. Shape chicken wire around the framework, and cover it with moss. Tie the moss in place with monofilament fishing line and you're set. If you like, you can form an indentation in the seat area and line it with plastic, then add potting soil and trailing plants, such as baby's tears (*Soleirolia soleirolii*). A topiary like this needs bright light, but must be kept out of direct sun. If you mist it regularly and water it carefully, it will stay healthy and attractive for years.

UP AGAINST THE WALL

The summer I was eight years old, my sister and I cajoled our parents into letting us sleep out in the backyard. Dad rigged an old green tarpaulin into a tent, and all afternoon long, Debbie and I carried out supplies and equipment—snacks, blankets, pillows, flashlights, even our toothbrushes. As darkness fell, we pulled on our baby-doll pajamas and lay at the tent opening, listening to the night sounds and watching the stars appear. We made shadow puppets in the flashlight beams and told each other every ghost story we knew. Eventually, we drifted off to sleep.

Shortly afterward, Dad gently shook us awake and herded us back to the house, explaining that we were much too frightened to sleep. Although we often spent the early evening in our tent that summer, we never again tried to spend the night there. Years later, Dad confessed that he and Mom had spent the whole time standing guard from their bedroom window. When Mom got tired and we hadn't yet retreated to the house, she dispatched him to explain our fears to us and insist that we come inside where we were safe.

If the romance of sleeping outside still calls to you, this headboard will give you the feeling of sleeping beneath a garden wall without keeping your mom and dad up all night.

1 Clamp two cedar 4 × 4s (10 × 10 cm) together and mark cutting lines for the dadoes as shown in the diagram on page 48. Set the cutting depth on a circular saw to exactly match the thickness of the 2 × 4 (5 × 10 cm) stringers. Between the lines marked for the dadoes, make cuts across the posts, one cut every

¼" (6 mm). Use a chisel to remove the waste material within the dadoes. Set the stringers into position, their ends flush with the outside edges of the posts and their faces flush with the faces of the posts. Secure the stringers with 2½" (6 cm) drywall screws.

2 Cut the plywood base and backing. Mark the

continued on page 48

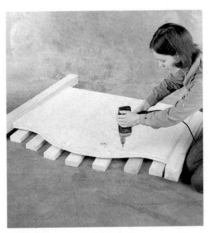

MATERIALS:
4 × 4 (10 × 10 CM) CEDAR POSTS (2) • ¾" (19 MM) PLYWOOD (1 SHEET)
• 2 × 4S (5 × 10 CM) (2) • 2½" (6 CM) DRYWALL SCREWS • LATEX UNDERLAYMENT
• MASKING TAPE • LATEX PAINT • 2 × 2" (5 × 5 CM) CERAMIC TILE
• TILE ADHESIVE • GROUT • LATEX ADDITIVE • DECK POST CAPS (2, OPTIONAL)
• GROUT SEALER • BOLTS • SEMI-GLOSS POLYURETHANE • HOLLYWOOD BED FRAME

setting lines for the tile on the base. Screw the base to the stringers and countersink the screws. Turn the assembly over and set the backing in place above the first stringer; align its edges with the edges of the base. Secure the backing by driving screws into it through the front of the base. Countersink the screws and fill the holes with latex underlayment. Mix paint into drywall compound at a ratio of 1:4. Mask off the tile area, including the top edge of the assembly. Using a drywall knife or 12" (30 cm) square-end trowel, spread the paint/wallboard compound mixture onto the unmasked portion of the base and backing, and then to the posts. Sweep across the compound, pressing down on one edge of the trowel or drywall knife to create a textured appearance. When the compound is completely dry, seal it with a coat of semi-gloss polyurethane.

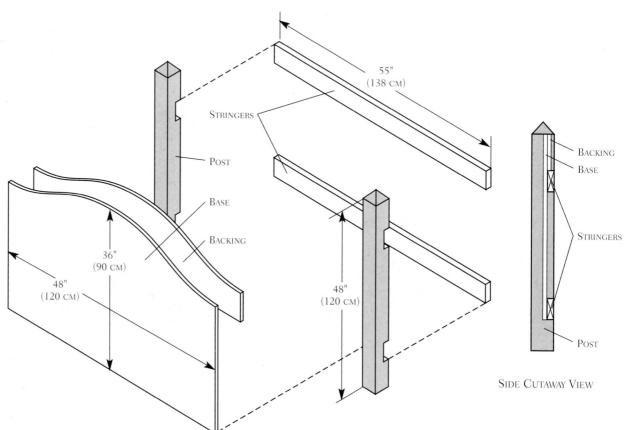

SIDE CUTAWAY VIEW

3 Lay out the tile and plan its placement. If necessary, use a tile cutter and nippers to trim the tile to fit.

4 Working on 18 to 24" (45 to 60 cm) at a time, spread tile adhesive on the top of the unfinished plywood of the base and backing. Set the field tile flush with the edge of the base and then the edge tile flush with the face of the field tile. Press each tile firmly into the adhesive, twisting the tile slightly to settle it in place.

5 When the tile adhesive is dry, mix grout and latex additive. Apply the grout, then wipe away the excess with a damp sponge. Rinse the sponge frequently and continue wiping until all the excess is removed. Let the grout dry for an hour, then polish the powdery film off of the tile. Allow the grout to cure as directed by the manufacturer before sealing it.

6 Mark and drill holes in the posts, then use bolts to attach a Hollywood bed frame to the headboard. Optional: Paint deck-post caps to complement the textured surface and add one to each post.

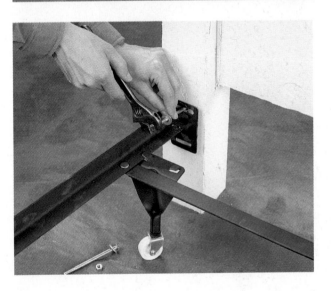

PIPE DREAMS

During the course of our first book collaboration, *Building Garden Ornaments*, Tim and I became interested in copper pipe as a building material. We're still intrigued by its adaptability and the number of ways different types and sizes of pipe and fittings can be put together. The combinations that produce this attractive headboard actually are very simple. We estimate it would take only two or three days to build and would cost under $100.

1 Following the diagram on page 52, cut all the rigid copper pieces to length. Mark the holes on the middle (¾" [19 mm]) and lower (1¼" [3 cm]) rails; centerpunch and drill ½" (12 mm) holes through only the first wall of each rail. On each upper post, mark the holes for the middle rail. Next, centerpunch the hole locations and then drill a ¾" (19 mm) hole through only the first wall of each upper post.

2 Lay out the middle and lower rails, and fit the braces between them. If necessary, use a rotary tool to tailor the holes until the pieces fit securely. Make sure the braces extend as far as possible into the rails—they support and strengthen them. Next, con-

struct each post by using a 1¼" (3 cm) tee to connect the upper and lower post pieces. Finally, connect the rail and brace assembly to the posts. Insert the middle rail into the hole on each post and the lower rail into the tee on each side. Make sure the middle rail extends as far as possible into the posts. Top each post with a 1¼ × ½" (30 × 12 mm) reducer and put a 1¼" (3 cm) end cap on the bottom of each.

3 Cut a 6-ft. (1.8 m) piece of ½" (12 mm) flexible copper for the upper rail. At one end, form an arc with a 5" (12 cm) radius, and then insert the end of the arc into the reducer at the top of one of the posts. At the other end, shape an arc that brings the end of the rail down to meet the reducer fitting on the second post. Trim the ends so the legs of the arcs are of equal length and the rail sits level across the headboard.

4 Clean and flux the joints, then dry-fit the pieces on a level, flame-resistant sur-

MATERIALS:

½" (12 MM) RIGID COPPER (12 FT. [3.6 M])
• ¾" (19 MM) RIGID COPPER (5 FT. [1.5 M])
• 1¼" (3 CM) RIGID COPPER (12 FT. [3.6 M])
• ½" (12 MM) FLEXIBLE COPPER (APPROX. 8 FT. [2.4 M])
• 1¼ × ½" (30 × 12 MM) COPPER REDUCERS (2)
• 1¼" (3 CM) COPPER END CAPS (2)
• 1¼" (3 CM) COPPER TEES
• ¼" (6 MM) COPPER TUBING (10-FT. [3 M] ROLL)
• HOLLYWOOD BED FRAME • NUTS & BOLTS
• 12-GAUGE (2MM) WIRE

face. Solder the joints, working from the bottom of the head-board and alternating from side to side. Check from time to time to make sure the assembly remains square and flat. (For more information on soldering, see page 127.)

5 To form the scrollwork: Cut two 30" (75 cm) pieces of ¼" (6 mm) copper tubing. Flatten both ends of one piece of tubing. Use locking pliers to clamp one end of the tubing to the top edge of a one-gallon paint can. Wrap about 15" (38 cm) of the tubing around the paint can, then remove it and reclamp the end to a piece of 1½" (4 cm) PVC pipe. Rotate the pipe to curl about 4" (10 cm) of the copper around the pipe, not quite one full rotation. Clamp the opposite end of the tubing to the PVC pipe and curl another 4" (10 cm). Repeat with the second 30" (75 cm) piece of tubing, checking after each step to make sure it matches the first.

6 Mark the center point of the upper and middle rails and set the first scroll between them. Unroll the tubing into a graceful curve that allows the large end of the scroll to align with the center point of the headboard and the small end to contact the middle rail about 6" (15 cm) from the post. Repeat

UPPER RAIL

1¼" × ½" (31 × 12 MM) REDUCER

MIDDLE RAIL 51" (128 CM)

BRACES 20½" (51 CM)

UPPER POST 21¼" (53 CM)

LOWER POST 16" (40 CM)

LOWER RAIL 49" (123 CM)

END CAP

this process to form the opposite scroll.

7 Flatten both ends of two 12" (30 cm) and two 6" (15 cm) pieces of ¼" (6 mm) tubing. Curl one end of each 12" (30 cm) piece around the PVC pipe and unwind it to form a gentle curve that contacts the middle rail about 2" (5 cm) from the post and reaches to a point about 6" (15 cm) beyond the small end of the original scroll. Curl each 6" (15 cm) piece around the 1½" (4 cm) piece of PVC pipe, and unwind it to repeat the pattern of the small end of the original scroll. Set this piece in place to contact the original scroll just before the end of the 12" (30 cm) scroll described above. (It does not contact the upper rail.) Repeat this process to complete the scrollwork on the opposite side of the headboard.

8 Clean and flux the contact spots on the tubing and upper and middle rails. Solder the tubing into position. Wrap 12-gauge (2 mm) wire around the tubing, forming 1" (2.5 cm) coils that conceal the joints.

9 Drill holes through each post and use nuts and bolts to secure a Hollywood frame to the headboard.

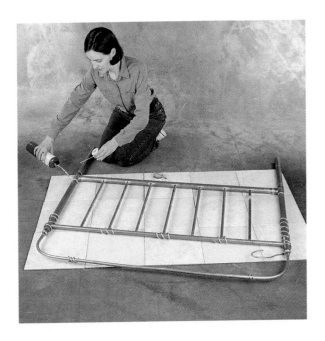

PERSONALITY

Gardens are as individual as the people who plant and care for them. In that same way, garden-style rooms reflect the interests and personalities of the people who live in them. For example, a bench supported by clay pots, such as the one shown above, or a table made from a stack of pots, such as the one shown on page 60, is especially appropriate in the home of an enthusiastic container gardener.

If you're passionate about a topic or a hobby, chances are you've gathered possessions that reflect your passion. To incorporate those themed possessions into your rooms, build or buy furnishings that complement them or allow you to display them effectively. Be careful not to get too much of a good thing, though. The furnishings and accessories in the sunroom at right indicate that someone in the family is interested in birds and their habitats, but only a few pieces are actually shaped like birdhouses. The casual style and natural materials of the other furnishings and accessories support the theme without overwhelming the room.

MATERIALS

Metals, which have a long history of use in gardens, earn a place in garden-style rooms as well. The graceful, intricate shapes of wire and wrought iron furniture blend well with the more solid surfaces of natural materials, such as wood and stone in the patio at left. In the bedroom above, the gleam of the iron bed provides a nice counterpoint to the weathered wood and stone accessories.

SCREENED OFF

Open floor plans, which are increasingly popular, are wonderful in many ways. But sometimes a space needs to be defined or separated for one reason or another. This simple screen is a perfect solution.

1 Cut and prepare the copper pipe for the frames. Dry-fit the pieces and then solder the joints, starting at the bottom and working toward the top. Don't solder the lower crosspieces to the frames. Note: The center frame has hinge extensions on both sides.

2 Cut three 68" (170 cm) lengths of canvas. Mask off the trellis pattern and paint the background. When the paint is completely dry, stencil a trompe l'oeil onto the canvas. Next, run a bead of silicone caulk along the top crosspiece. Press the canvas into the caulk and clamp it in place. When the caulk is dry, wrap the fabric around the crosspiece. Run a bead of caulk along the lower crosspiece and clamp the canvas into place. When that caulk is dry, use a pair of locking pliers to turn the crosspiece within the fittings until the canvas is wrapped around the pipe and the fabric is taut across the frame. Drill four evenly spaced pilot holes across each crosspiece and secure the canvas to the pipe with steel pop rivets.

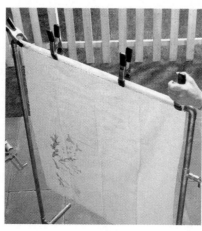
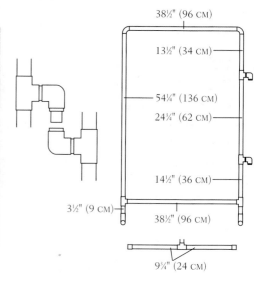

MATERIALS:

¾" (19 MM) COPPER PIPE (60 FT. [18 M]) • ¾" (19 MM) COPPER TEES (20)
• ¾" (19 MM) COPPER END CAPS (12) • ¾" (19 MM) COPPER 90° ELBOWS (14)
• ⅝ × ¾" (15 × 19 MM) BRASS FLANGE BEARINGS (8) • CANVAS • MASKING TAPE • PAINT • STENCIL
• SILICONE CAULK • STEEL POP RIVETS

POTTING IT TOGETHER

There's a perpetual stash of damaged clay pots in the corner of my garage. Like most gardeners, I use the shards to create drainage in the bottom of container plantings, but the supply always seems to exceed the demand. If you have broken pots around, you can put them to good use in the mosaic bands on the pots supporting this table.

You can buy pre-cut glass tabletops in many stores; you can also have a top cut to size. Tell the shop personnel how you plan to use the glass and follow their recommendations regarding thickness, size, and type of glass.

1▸ Mask off the rims of two clean, dry 17" (43 cm) clay pots. Prime the pots and three pot feet and let them dry. On each, brush on a thin coat of umber acrylic paint and let it dry. Dilute some gold acrylic paint with clear glaze and brush it on lightly—let some umber show through. Let the pots dry, then spray acrylic sealer onto the painted portions.

2▸ Put the damaged pots into a paper bag and use a rubber mallet to break them. Hot glue the shards and bits of sea glass to the unpainted strip on the pots. When the glue is set, grout the mosaic, using a sponge to push the grout into the open spaces. Wipe away the excess grout, using a damp sponge. Rinse the sponge often and keep wiping until you've removed all the grit. When the grout

dries, polish the surface with a clean, dry cloth.

3▸ Stack the pots and run a bead of silicone caulk around the edges. Thread washers and a bolt through the drainage holes to connect the pots, then set the column onto the pot feet. Add rubber bumpers and set the glass in place.

MATERIALS:
MASKING TAPE • 17" (43 CM) CLAY POTS (2) • POT FEET (3) • ACRYLIC PAINT • CLEAR GLAZE
• CLEAR MATTE ACRYLIC SEALER • HOT GLUE • GROUT • SILICONE CAULK
• 2" (5 CM) MACHINE BOLT AND NUT • METAL WASHERS (2)
• RUBBER BUMPERS • GLASS TABLETOP

LEAFING OUT

Gardeners have a love affair with leaves. We're often drawn to plants based on the color, shape, or texture of their leaves. We pay special attention when shoots peek out of the soil in spring; when the trees begin to bud in earnest; when the flaming sumacs tell us it's time to begin preparing the garden for winter. Our fascination with leaves makes them important motifs in garden style.

1 Enlarge the pattern below. (Many copy centers have blueprint copiers and staff members who can help you reproduce the pattern to scale.) Use a pounce wheel to transfer the pattern onto the plywood, then cut out the tabletop. Cut a circle of plywood to match the diameter of the arms of your pedestal base. Mark the center of the tabletop and of the plywood circle. Match those centers and attach the circle to the tabletop with 1½" (4 cm) screws driven down through the top. Fill the screw holes and any voids in the edges of the plywood with lightweight spackle. When dry, lightly sand the spackle.

2 Paint a basecoat onto the table. Add details as indicated on the pattern.

3 Install the pedestal base by driving 2" (5 cm) screws up through the holes in the pedestal and into the plywood circle and tabletop.

MATERIALS:
¾" (19 MM) PLYWOOD • 1½" (4 CM) SCREWS • PAINTS • 2" (5 CM) SCREWS • PATTERN
• TABLE BASE • POUNCE WHEEL • SPACKLE

PLANTS AND FLOWERS

I think plants and flowers make almost any space look brighter, more attractive, and more interesting. Of course, as a gardener, I can hardly be considered objective.

My dad often says of me, "The only way that girl knows how to go at something is like she's killing snakes." He means that I tend to get carried away. When I first decided to establish a perennial garden, I ripped out the shrubs in front of half my house. Then I hauled 12 tons of landscape gravel out of the area and dumped it at the far back edge of the yard, by the marsh. I forced myself to shovel up and haul away at least ten wheelbarrow loads of gravel each day. The afternoon that I moved the last wheelbarrow load of gravel, I opened a bottle of champagne and toasted the accomplishment.

In a book on perennial gardening, I discovered the concept of soil amendment. In typical fashion, I ordered a dump-truck load of black dirt the very next morning and hauled home a trailer load of compost and a dozen bales of peat moss. It took a week to place and till it to my satisfaction.

Since I was a rank beginner, I ordered a perennial collection from a mail-order nursery, complete with planting diagrams. The day the plants arrived, I leaped into action. My daughter came home from a friend's house at 10:30 that night to find me kneeling in the beam of a large flashlight, patting the very last plant into place. She looked around and said, "This looks great, Mom. When are you going to do the rest?" I lay right down on the ground and laughed until I cried.

In a garden, plants and flowers are the focal point, but they can receive the same attention indoors as well. In the sunny space at left, pots are packed together in a small area to produce the sense of a border. To arrange an indoor border, start by putting the largest plants in the back and graduate to smaller ones in front. Include flowering plants as well as foliage in a wide range of colors, textures, and leaf sizes.

In the breakfast nook shown above, the plants lead your attention around the room. Plant stands and other furnishings are used to bring the greenery up to eye level throughout the room, a strategy that helps emphasize the windows and window treatments.

BREAKING THEM IN

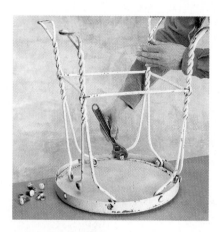

Tim's mother once came in from hanging out the wash to find three-year-old Tim and his four-year-old sister, Joy, hurling her best china at the dining room buffet. They were having a great time, laughing at the clatter they were making as the dishes broke and the buffet rocked. Tim's folks still have that scarred buffet, and Tim and Joy still hear its tale at family gatherings.

No matter how your dishes get broken, you can use them in a simple mosaic that transforms an ordinary ice cream parlor chair into something special.

1 *Loosen the bolts holding the chair bottom, and remove the plywood and upholstery materials. Hold the plywood in place and trace the outline of the chair frame onto it.*

2 *Now you're ready to break the plates. If you're trying to preserve a center medallion, put masking tape across the back of the plate. Place each plate in a paper bag and tap it gently but firmly with a rubber mallet. Use tile nippers to refine the pieces. Glue the pieces to the plywood. (Keep all the pieces within the outline of the chair frame.)*

3 *Replace the plywood base in the frame and tighten the bolts. Apply grout to the mosaic, filling all the voids around the pieces and at the edges. Use a damp sponge to clean away excess grout. Rinse the sponge frequently and continue wiping until the surface is clean. Several hours later, remove the grout film by polishing the mosaic with a dry cloth.*

MATERIALS:

WIRE ICE CREAM PARLOR CHAIR • CHINA PLATES
• SILICONE GLUE • GROUT

BENCHED

Salvaged lumber has a romance about it—the wood itself holds memories and stories. When I was a kid, my dad rescued some walnut boards from my great-grandpa's barn. We hauled those boards, tied to the top of a '59 Ford, from south-central Iowa to California. Just before the state line, Dad rigged a way to hide them under the car so we could get them through California's border patrol—the only illegal thing I ever saw my father do. It was worth the effort: Each piece Dad built from that lumber is a treasure.

If you have or can find salvaged lumber to go with the old window sash for this potting bench, it will add another dimension to the project. If not, you could "weather" cedar lumber to achieve nearly the same effect. All you need to do is dissolve baking soda in hot water, about 1 part baking soda to 5 parts water. Spray the solution onto the boards and set them in bright sunlight—they'll turn a lovely shade of gray.

continued on page 70

MATERIALS:

SALVAGED WINDOW SASH • 1½" (38 MM) WOOD SCREWS • 1¼" (31 MM) WOOD SCREWS • ½" (12 MM) WOOD SCREWS • 2" (5 CM) WOOD SCREWS • ½" (12 MM) PLYWOOD • ANGLE IRON • PLANTING BASIN • 2 × 4 (5 × 10 CM) LUMBER • 1 × 4 (2.5 × 10 CM) LUMBER • 1 × 2 (2.5 × 5 CM) LUMBER • 1 × 6 (2.5 × 15 CM) LUMBER

1 Measure the window sash. Lay out the two 2 × 4 (5 × 10 cm) back legs and determine where to position the braces, based on the dimensions of the sash. Drill pilot holes and attach both 1 × 4 (2.5 × 10 cm) horizontal braces and then the 1 × 2 (2.5 × 5 cm) vertical sash braces, using 1½" (38 mm) wood screws. Use angle iron and ½" (12 mm) wood screws to attach the 1 × 6 (2.5 × 15 cm) ledge, flush with the back of the lower horizontal brace. On the back face of the back legs, add the 1 × 4 (2.5 × 10 cm) lower back horizontal brace, driving the screws from the front of the brace.

2 Assemble the 2 × 4 (5 × 10 cm) front legs and 1 × 4 (2.5 × 10 cm) upper and lower side braces, using 2" (5 cm) wood screws. Attach these assemblies to the back frame, securing the upper side braces to the outside edge of the back legs with 2" (5 cm) wood screws.

3 Attach the upper front brace and then add the mid-table brace. Attach the lower front brace.

4 Lay the 1 × 6 (2.5 × 15 cm) decking on the lower shelf, securing each piece with pairs of screws driven into each lower side brace. Next, lay the 1 × 6 (2.5 × 15 cm) decking on the tabletop, driving pairs of screws into each upper side brace as well as the mid-table brace. Measure the planting basin; cut a square piece of ½" (12 mm) plywood, 4" (10 cm) larger than the circumference of the basin. Trace the basin onto the plywood, and use a jig saw to cut out the hole. Position this plywood brace to indicate the hole for the planting basin, and trace the cutout onto the decking. From below, attach the plywood to the underside of the decking, driving two 1¼" (31 mm) wood screws through the brace and into each decking board. Use a jig saw to cut along the marked lines to make the hole in the decking for the planting basin.

5 Set the window into position and secure it to the horizontal braces, using 2" (5 cm) wood screws.

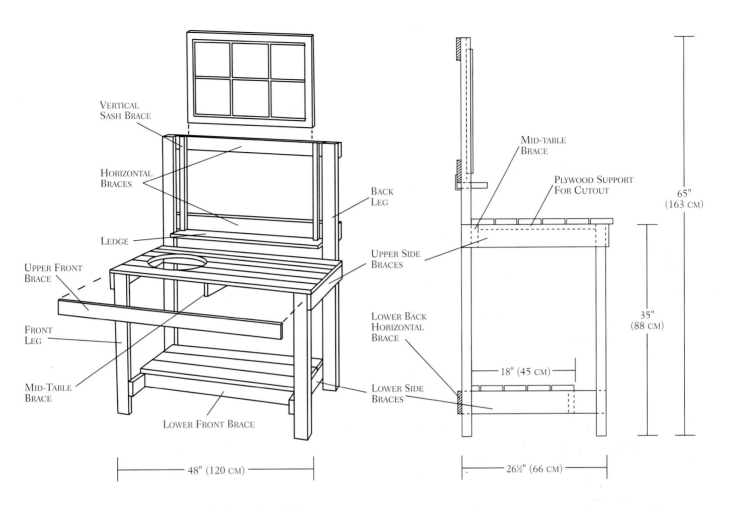

VERTICAL
SASH BRACE

HORIZONTAL
BRACES

LEDGE

UPPER FRONT
BRACE

FRONT
LEG

MID-TABLE
BRACE

LOWER FRONT BRACE

BACK
LEG

UPPER SIDE
BRACES

LOWER BACK
HORIZONTAL
BRACE

LOWER SIDE
BRACES

MID-TABLE
BRACE

PLYWOOD SUPPORT
FOR CUTOUT

65"
(163 CM)

35"
(88 CM)

18" (45 CM)

48" (120 CM)

26½" (66 CM)

STICK TO IT

Tim's been building things with sticks since he and his brother cut willow twigs from the banks of Wisconsin's Sugar River to make little rafts. They'd drop the rafts—which included huts and flag poles—from a bridge and watch them float away down the river.

Tim put his stick experience to good use in designing this little chair. Of course, it's not meant to be used for seating, just to create a woodsy, garden effect.

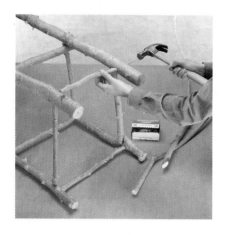

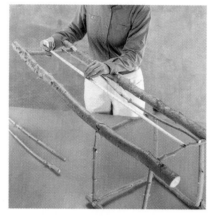

1 Before you begin, review the techniques for building with twigs on page 132. Cut the branches and the seat as indicated on the drawing below. Drill pilot holes, and nail the horizontal supports in place. Do the same with the back legs and supports. Measure between the legs and cut additional supports to fit.

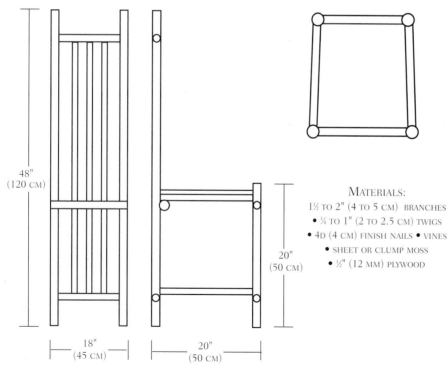

48"
(120 CM)

20"
(50 CM)

18"
(45 CM)

20"
(50 CM)

MATERIALS:
1½ TO 2" (4 TO 5 CM) BRANCHES
• ¼ TO 1" (2 TO 2.5 CM) TWIGS
• 4D (4 CM) FINISH NAILS • VINES
• SHEET OR CLUMP MOSS
• ½" (12 MM) PLYWOOD

2 4" (10 cm) from the top and bottom of the back leg/supports, measure between the branches. Cut horizontal supports to fit. Then cut four twigs to fit and tack them in place, extending the length of the back.

3 Cut a plywood seat, nail it in place, and hot glue moss to cover it.

CONTRAST

When you're working with backgrounds and furnishings in a limited range of color, use shape and texture to provide contrast. In the breakfast room above, worn painted finishes, weathered metal, and lace curtains keep the room interesting despite the mostly neutral color scheme. In the dining room at right, the fanciful shapes of the chairs, the textures of the fabrics, and the pattern of the rug work in much the same way. In both rooms, plants and flowers add lively spots of color.

ADAPTATION

Gardeners are experts at recycling—think compost here. Truly, finding new ways to use things is at the very heart of garden style. In the sunny bedroom at left, a window sash has been converted into a mirror, and a chenille bedspread and some vintage fabrics have metamorphosed into charming throw pillows.

In some cases, finding a piece is only half the fun—the other half is adapting it to a practical purpose. You do need to think carefully before you make any changes to vintage treasures. If there's any chance you might be preparing to destroy the value of an antique or rare primitive piece, stop in your tracks. Consult an expert before you do anything you could later regret.

Most of the time, you won't have to worry about making that kind of mistake. The price you paid for the piece will guide you and so will its condition. Let's say, for example, you found a dresser such as this one, in great shape except for a ruined top. Clearly, the top would have to be refinished or replaced anyway, so the decision to alter it is not one you have to agonize over. From there, it's not much of a leap to decide to paint it or even replace the hardware.

If you don't have much experience with do-it-yourself projects, do some research before you begin. Don't be intimidated; you can do just about anything that could be required to adapt a piece to your purposes. Start at a bookstore or library. There are many good books available to help you learn to finish or refinish wood, produce a variety of painted finishes, or do a broad range of typical repairs. Most of these projects won't require anything beyond a few tools, a little patience, and a good dose of common sense. (My mother says that the least common thing in the world is common sense. While that may be true, we can all develop some if we apply ourselves.)

If you don't have the time or any interest in doing these projects yourself, develop a network of people you can turn to for help. There are few people more useful to know than a good carpenter; a skilled woodworker could be helpful, too.

FENCED IN

Many of us have associated picket fences with gardens since we were kids. When we read about Peter Rabbit getting his buttons caught in Mr. McGregor's fence, or dreamed of vine-covered cottages, or maybe when we visited our grandmother's gardens, picket fences were part of the picture. This picket fence shelf lends an air of nostalgia to whatever is displayed there. Mine holds a treasured collection of pictures of my children, Evan and Katie, and the artwork they've done over the years.

To create a weathered appearance, we used two colors of paint and a crackle medium. It's best to choose colors with a fair amount of contrast so that the cracks reveal a basecoat that's decidedly different from the topcoat.

When you hang the shelf, drive screws into the wall studs or use hollow wall anchors to support the weight of the shelf.

1 *Buy a section of standard picket fence and cut it to size. Or, if you prefer a picket style that's not available pre-fabricated, you can cut your own pickets and stringers and build a fence section.*

2 *Paint both sides and top and bottom of the fence section, the brackets, and the shelves with a coat of latex paint. When that's completely dry, add a coat of crackle medium. When the crackle medium is dry, add another coat of latex paint—cracks will appear as the paint dries.*

3 *Center each shelf on the fence section; mark the placement of the brackets. Drive screws into the pickets and then attach the brackets to the front of the fence. Add hanging hardware to the back, hang the unit, and set the shelves in place.*

MATERIALS:
SECTION OF PICKET FENCE • LATEX PAINT (2 COLORS)
• CRACKLE MEDIUM • PRE-FAB SHELF WITH BRACKETS
• 1" (2.5 CM) DRYWALL SCREWS • HANGING HARDWARE

APPLE LADDER

When my children were younger, every autumn included a trip to the apple orchard with friends. It was always an adventure—calming excited little ones, shooing the bees homing in on sticky hands and cheeks, counting noses for the trip home. I looked forward to it each year and now miss those days.

For me, this apple ladder is a quiet reminder of those trips. The traditional version is 7 or 8 (2 to 2.5 m) feet tall, and wider at the base than at the top. This is a case where form truly follows function—the shape of the ladder is perfectly suited to leaning into a tree laden with fruit. Indoors, an apple ladder can support a collection of hanging plants in a kitchen or family room, or it can display quilts, towels, or vintage linens in a bedroom or bathroom. During the holidays, you might even set it in a corner and suspend a collection of unique ornaments from its upper rungs.

1 Cut two 72" (1.8 m) 1 × 4s (2.5 × 10 cm). Mark and cut a 10° angle at one end and an 80° angle at the other of each board. On each board, center a mark 10½" (26 cm) from one end; make four more marks, each one 14" (35 cm) from the other. Using a 1" (2.5 cm) hole saw, cut one hole at each mark.

2 Cut five rungs from a 1¼" (3 cm) dowel, 26", 22½", 19¼", 16", and 12½" (65, 56, 48, 40, and 31 cm) long. Arrange the rungs so that the ladder narrows as it reaches the top. Glue the dowels into the holes and tack them into place, angling the nails down through the legs and into the dowels. Paint or stain the ladder as desired.

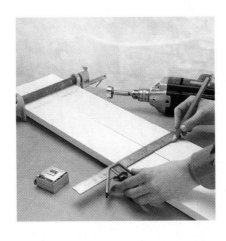

MATERIALS:
PINE 1×4S (2.5 × 10 CM) (2) • 1¼" (3 CM) WOOD DOWEL (8 FT. [2.5 M])
• WOOD GLUE • 6D (5 CM) FINISH NAILS • PAINT OR STAIN

THANKS FOR THE MEMORIES

Tim's a packrat. He came by it naturally—his grandfather saved every receipt he ever received. They filled a five-drawer file. Tim himself keeps an enormous memory album of ticket stubs, expired driver's licenses, student IDs, even one gum wrapper. (I'm dying to know the story of that gum wrapper, but when I ask, Tim just smiles.)

Although most of us don't go to those extremes, we do like to keep mementos—invitations, cards, tickets, photos. This ribbon board provides attractive display space for just those sorts of things.

1 Remove the mirror from the frame. Clean, sand, and paint the frame. Measure the opening and cut a piece of ⅜" (9 mm) plywood to fit.

2 Cut quilt batting 2" (5 cm) larger than the plywood; cut fabric 3" (7.5 cm) larger. Layer the fabric (right side down), the batting, and the plywood. Wrap the fabric and batting around the plywood, keeping the fabric taut and the grain straight; staple the fabric in place.

3 Arrange the ribbons, pull them taut, and tack them in place. Cut each ribbon to extend about 1" (2.5 cm) beyond the fabric on the back, then turn the board over and staple the ribbons in place.

4 Insert a tack at selected intersections, then hot glue a button to each tack. Toenail the finished board into the mirror frame. Add hanging hardware.

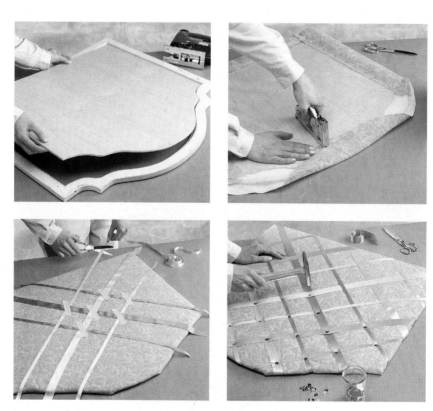

MATERIALS:

MIRROR FRAME • LATEX PAINT • ⅜" (9 MM) PLYWOOD • QUILT BATTING • FABRIC • TACKS • RIBBONS
• ANTIQUE BUTTONS • HOT GLUE • HANGING HARDWARE

$\mathscr{A}$CCESSORIES

Accessories are the annuals of a decorating scheme. Like annuals, they change with the seasons and so are free to put all their energies into display. They provide bursts of color and evidence of your wit and personality.

Gardeners seem to have an innate respect for history and heredity, so personal mementos have a natural place in garden-style rooms. Take those old photos out of their boxes or albums and frame them; get out the kids' art projects and see if you can find the ones you did when you were young. If you're a collector, pull out your collections and give them places of honor throughout your home.

From there, begin to make use of odds and ends that relate to gardening. Pull masses of houseplants together to imitate a border; turn old bottles and jars into vases and candleholders; convert a stack of rose-covered teacups into a lamp. You could suspend a sturdy trellis from the ceiling and use it as a pot rack, or prop it against a wall and use it to display bunches of dried flowers.

The most important thing is to engage your imagination and use accessories that please you. Don't worry about what's in style or how other people decorate. A copper-roofed martin house stands on a pedestal in a corner of my dining room. You wouldn't believe how many friends have offered to help me put it in the yard, but there it stays—offbeat and charming. I recently met someone who had fashioned antique garden shears into a sculpture that he used in place of a traditional mantle. Certainly out of the ordinary, but entirely wonderful.

The best advice is simple: Have fun.

Accessories have more impact when they're arranged so you see them as a group rather than as random objects. This idea is carried out in both rooms shown here. The pieces are not only grouped, they're integrated into a scene.

Arranging accessories is a lot like composing a still life, and you can follow some of the same principles. The area that you're accessorizing basically acts as the background, and what you're trying to do is to create an interesting balance between the accessories and the spaces that surround them.

The first thing to do is collect all the objects. Whether you're creating a new arrangement or significantly changing an existing one, put all the pieces on the floor or a table and spend some time studying the various sizes and shapes you plan to use. When I create a new arrangement, I usually scatter the things around me and look at them until something speaks to me as a starting point. Typically you'll want to put the largest objects in the back, so it often makes sense to start with those. Keep trying out possible arrangements until something jells. Don't worry—you'll recognize it when it happens.

Be careful not to crowd the composition. It's a good idea to overlap a few pieces, but you need to make sure you can see each object clearly. Just like in a painting, you want certain elements to lead your eye into and around the image you're creating. In the dining room shown at right, the entire room is treated as a composition. The chandelier draws your eye to the composition; the center platter commands attention; and the positions of the remaining pieces, including the handles on the cups, lead you around the arrangement and then back down to the fireplace.

When Tim and I are working on a project design and I start fretting over the placement of one element or another, he reminds me of what he calls the "rule of thirds." That's his favorite way of describing a pleasing spatial relationship. Boiled down to its essence, it means that if you're going to overlap two objects, do it by about a third. If you're going to stagger two objects, place the top of one about a third of the way down from the top of the other. There are more complex theories and rules for composition, but you can't go wrong by following Tim's rule of thirds.

HANGING AROUND

A couple of hours spent in the aisles of a neighborhood hardware store can have unforeseen results. Until it caught my eye from a display of plumbing materials, I had no idea how flexible and useful aluminum tubing could be. Like silver solder, it's inexpensive and really easy to shape. Here we use both materials to suspend vases in unusual ways. Once you get the idea, let your imagination take wing with new shapes and creations.

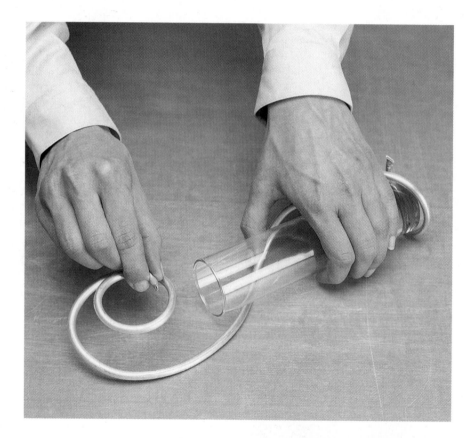

Aluminum Tubing: *Shape ¼" (6 mm) aluminum tubing around a tall, cylindrical vase. Be sure the shaped tubing forms a base that will support the weight of the vase. At the top of the vase, form a graceful hanging loop. Hang the vase from a small crystal knob or other decorative hanger.*

Silver Solder: *Use wooden dowels of various sizes to shape silver solder into spirals and decorative shapes. Drape a loop of solder over the top of the bottle to act as a hanging loop; use loops of solder or wire to hold the hanging loop in place. Add wire accents or decorative beads.*

MATERIALS:

ALUMINUM TUBING • VASE
• SILVER SOLDER • DOWELS • BOTTLES
• SMALL CRYSTAL DOOR KNOB

ALL IT COULD BE

Tim and I look at objects differently from most people—we generally see things for what they are and for what they could be. When Tim spied this flowermarket can, he saw it as the basis for an artistic watering can.

The construction is simple enough that anyone can do it, but I don't know another living soul who could have contrived the ingenious combination that produced this piece. Have fun with it!

1 Cut 36" (90 cm) of copper tubing; use a rubber mallet to flatten the first 4" (10 cm) of one end. Clamp the flattened end to a #12 garden pail and form a circle. Refine the circle into a handle that fits the flower can. Now, cut away the lower three-quarters of a ½" (12 mm) tee fitting, then drill a ⅛" (3 mm) hole in each remaining tab. Also drill two ⅛" (3 mm) holes at the flattened end of the handle.

2 Form an open "S" shape from a 30" (75 cm) piece of copper tubing; trim one end square and the other at an angle—the final result should be 24" (60 cm) long. Solder a ½" (12 mm) brass flare fitting to the square-cut end. Fold a 32" (80 cm) piece of 8-gauge (4 mm) copper wire in half, maintaining a 1" (25 mm) arc at the fold. On the can, draw two reference lines opposite each other and 90° from the seam. At one line, mark and drill a ½" (12 mm) hole ¾" (19 mm) up from the bottom of the can. Then drill four 3/16" (5 mm) holes ⅜" (9 mm) down from the rim and ½" (12 mm) on either side of the remaining reference line.

3 Assemble the handle and fittings; drill holes and attach the handle with ⅛" (3 mm) aluminum rivets. Lightly solder the handle and fittings in place. Thread the ends of the stay through the holes and make a 90° bend ⅜" (9 mm) from the end of each. Rest the angled end of the spout in the loop of the stay and thread the other end through the can; use a ring nut and silicone sealant to secure it. Lightly solder the point where the spout and the stay meet. From the inside, seal all rivet locations with silicone.

MATERIALS:

COPPER TUBING • GARDEN PAIL
• ¼" (6 MM) BRASS FLARE FITTING
• COPPER WIRE • ALUMINUM RIVETS
• RING NUT • SILICON SEALANT
• ½" (12 MM) TEE FITTING

Shaping Up

Few things say "garden" like shaped shrubs—just put one into a room and watch the ambience change. The only problem is that topiaries typically are quite expensive. Don't let that stop you. With masking tape, a pair of pruners, and a basic shrub, you can make your own.

A topiary such as this can live in a bright room for three to four weeks at a time, but then it will need to spend some time out-doors. While it's indoors, mist it often and water it regularly. Prune your topiary each spring. Protect it from strong sunlight for its first few weeks and after each touch-up.

1 *Choose a full, cone-shaped conifer. (We used a Dwarf Alberta Spruce, Picea glauco 'Conica'.) Wind tape around the tree in a spiral. The tape will be a cutting guide, and the goal is to divide the tree into three sections that get thicker toward the base.*

2 *Starting at the top, cut back the branches just above and below the tape. Work slowly and clip only a little at a time until you see the spiral begin to take shape.*

3 *Remove the tape. Trim the remaining branches to rein-force the shape and create smooth, round edges for the spiral.*

MATERIALS:

CONIFER • MASKING TAPE

WHIMSY

Think of adding accessories as an opportunity to incorporate your favorite colors, to introduce unexpected patterns, and to include textures that please you. As you're scouting for accessories, remember that in the finished room you won't see one item at a time—each piece will always be seen in the context of its surroundings.

The bedroom at left includes a mixture of comforts and curiosities. I particularly enjoy the tea table set for the doll and teddy bear, and the dried flowers hanging from the headboard and window treatments. Unusual touches like these reveal the personality and creative flair that set a room apart and make it special.

The plant containers shown above are another example of personal flair. Not everyone would think of using tin cans as planters, but in combination with the colorful flowers, they're quite striking.

PATIENCE

Gardens are built over time. So are garden-style rooms, and to be successful they must exude a sense of beloved objects acquired, built, and tended over time. In the vignette above, the stones, shells, and other bits and pieces look as though they've been collected on many different beaches over long years. Displayed together, they have the kind of homey charm that comes only from patiently gathered memorabilia.

The dried flowers displayed over the sink in the kitchen at right appear to be a mixture of favorites from the garden and sentimental keepsakes. Other accessories throughout the kitchen, such as the collection of vases, the antique seltzer bottle and cheerful fabrics, reflect the delightful pairing of old and new that is part of the character of well-loved gardens.

A FORMAL ARRANGEMENT

Like a garden, no garden room is complete without flowers. Cut, dried, silk, potted, hanging—all your favorites can be worked into the scheme of things.

1 Cut a 60" (1.5 m) length of wire and mark out twelve 3" (7.5 cm) spaces and two 6" (15 cm) tails. At each 3" (7.5 cm) mark, wrap the wire around a pencil to form a small loop. At the center of the wire, make a 90° bend for the point of the heart. At the top of the heart, bring the tails together and twist them together. Twist the remainder of each tail into a loop, one on each side of the heart.

2 Cut a foam block to fit inside the lower part of the wire frame. Cut short stems of leather leaf, lavender, and dried hydrangea; insert small groups of each into the sides of the block. Form a loop of bear grass, curl the ends, then hot glue it to the face of the block. Insert a rose through the center of the block and wire it in place. Glue sheet moss and additional stems of dried hydrangea to the block, filling any open areas around the rose. Hot glue this arrangement to the center of the framework. Add a ribbon for a hanging loop.

MATERIALS:

WIRE • FOAM BLOCK • LEAF STEMS • BEAR GRASS
• HOT GLUE • ROSE • SHEET MOSS • RIBBON

LIVING ART

Most young children love dandelions, and my daughter was no exception. Horrified to see me pulling her favorites from the lawn, she didn't agree that they were weeds. "The only difference between a weed and a flower," said my then-five-year-old philosopher, "is your opinion. Dandelions make the grass prettier."

The colors of this piece remind me of dandelions. And like Katie's favorites, it makes a room prettier.

1 Cut the plywood pieces as indicated in the drawing at left. Stack the pieces for the sides of the shadow box and drill a ⅛" (3 mm) hole through both. Assemble the shadow box, using wire brads and glue. Clamp the box together until the glue dries.

2 Run a bead of construction adhesive along the top edge of the shadow box and position it on the back of the frame. Let the adhesive dry, then paint or stain the outside of the finished box as you wish.

3 Cut the backing from ¼" (6 mm) acid-free foam board. Use spray fixative to secure handmade paper to the backing and to the inside faces of the shadow box. Form silver solder into loops for the vase holders; thread one end through each side of the shadow box and bend an angle to hold it in place. Add test tubes or small, cylindrical vases and fresh or silk flowers.

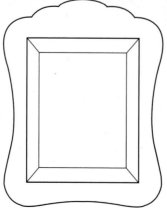

MATERIALS:

¼" (6 MM) PLYWOOD • WOOD GLUE • WIRE BRADS • CONSTRUCTION ADHESIVE • PAINT OR STAIN • FOAM BOARD
• SPRAY FIXATIVE • SILVER SOLDER • TEST TUBES OR VASES • FRESH OR SILK FLOWERS • HAND-MADE PAPER

PUYALLUP PUBLIC LIBRARY

PAILS OF POSIES

People of a certain age who spent time in rural areas probably have fond memories of buckets like these. I certainly do. One stood on a small table in the corner of my grandma's kitchen. From it we dipped the world's sweetest water for bean soup and iced tea and an endless stream of thick, black coffee for Grandpa. When the bucket was empty, a child was delegated to fill it at the pump out back.

With indoor running water available virtually everywhere nowadays, these buckets found new life as flower pots.

1 Poke some holes in a cake tin, using an awl or nail set. Set the tin (upside down) into the bottom of each bucket. Cover each tin with a piece of landscape fabric and a 2" (5 cm) layer of pea gravel. Add lightweight potting soil and plants.

2 Install a hook in the ceiling—use hardware designed to hold at least 25 pounds (11 kg), and be sure you hit a joist. Drill a hole about ½" (12 mm) from each end of a 13" (33 cm) piece of a hardwood 1 × 2 (2.5 × 5 cm). Run a rope around the pulley and thread one end through each hole in the board. Suspend the pulley from a chain attached to the hook, then tie one end of the rope to each bucket.

 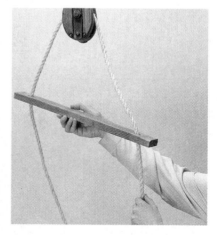

MATERIALS:

CAKE TINS (2) • BUCKETS (2) • LANDSCAPE FABRIC • PEA GRAVEL • POTTING SOIL • PLANTS
• CEILING HOOK • 1 × 2 (2.5 × 5 CM) HARDWOOD • PULLEY • ROPE • CHAIN

CONTAINING A GARDEN

Tim's mom kept a garden that stretched 80 feet (24 m) long and 25 feet (7.6 m) wide. Her garden produced the usual array of fruits and vegetables, but certain areas were designated for flowers, and the back row was always reserved for gladiolas. Tim remembers carrying enormous buckets and baskets of flowers up to the house at the end of a day's gardening.

Today's gardens typically are somewhat scaled down from the one Mrs. Himsel kept, but cutting gardens still fill our homes with flowers whenever possible. Baskets like these make nice additions to a garden room in any season, especially when the outdoor garden is dormant.

1 Cover the bottom of a wire basket with dry sphagnum moss. Tear off smaller pieces of moss and line the sides of the basket, arranging these pieces to overlap the moss on the bottom and extend to the top of the basket.

2 Cut a piece of landscape plastic to fit the basket. Cut X-shaped slits in the area that will sit at the bottom. Place the plastic over the moss and fill the basket with potting soil.

3 Place plants in the soil, loosening the root ball of each plant. Add potting soil around the plants, leaving at least ½" (12 mm) of space at the top for watering. Cover the spaces between the plants with pieces of moss to help keep the soil moist between waterings.

MATERIALS:

WIRE BASKET • SPAGHNUM MOSS
• 6 MIL PLASTIC • POTTING SOIL • PLANTS

FLOOR TO CEILING

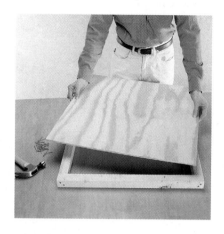

Tin ceiling tiles were originally developed as an economical alternative to elaborate European carved plasterwork. They were popular throughout North America from the mid-nineteenth century to the early twentieth, and as buildings and homes from that era have been torn down or remodeled, many of the tiles have been salvaged.

Whether painted, lacquered, or plated, these embossed panels are beautiful. They're also easy to work with and relatively inexpensive. We used a couple of panels to convert a simple wooden box into a striking planter.

1 Assemble 2 × 2 (5 × 5 cm) frames as shown in the illustration. Secure plywood to each frame, using glue and wood screws.

2 Join the frames into a box, and then add plywood to the bottom.

3 Run several beads of construction adhesive across the backs of the ceiling tiles, and then clamp them in place. Cut the 1 × 3s (2.5 × 7.5 cm) and corner trim; paint the 1 × 3s (2.5 × 7.5 cm), the corner trim, and the 2 × 2 (5 × 5 cm) at the top of each frame to match or complement your ceiling tiles. Drill pilot holes and nail the 1 × 3s (2.5 × 7.5 cm) to the bottom of the planter; add the corner trim in the same way.

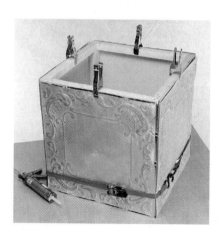

MATERIALS:

TIN CEILING TILE • 2 × 2s (5 × 5 cm) • ¼" (6 mm) PLYWOOD
• 1 × 3s (2.5 × 7.5 cm) • CONSTRUCTION ADHESIVE • WOOD GLUE
• 2½" (6 cm) WOOD SCREWS • PAINT OR STAIN • CORNER TRIM

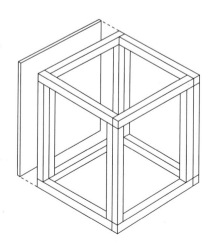

LIGHT

Light is as essential to a garden-style room as it is to the growth of plants. Although we can't live in rooms completely open to the sky, we can make the best possible use of available light and add candles and other touches of sparkle. In the family room above, the fabric swags are held well out of the way of the windows, and the shutters are set to filter the light and then direct it upward and into the room. The garden setting at right illustrates how effective a collection of candles can be in small spaces.

Candles, lamps, and chandeliers are very valuable accessories. You can use lighting to play tricks that improve the shape and proportion of a room, highlight an interesting detail, or disguise an ugly one. To make a ceiling look higher, use floor lamps or wall sconces that throw the light upward. On the other hand, keeping most of the lighting at lower levels reduces the appearance of height in a room. Positioning lamps or candles so they're reflected in mirrors at the end or side of a room makes the room appear to be deeper or wider, depending on their placement.

If a room includes valuable art or vintage fabrics, be especially careful about the type and placement of the lighting you use—some types of lighting can encourage fading or discoloration. Many lighting stores have specialists who can give you advice and guidance on this subject.

For most circumstances, the following guidelines will produce an effective lighting scheme: The lower edge of the shade on a table lamp should be at eye level when you're seated—about 38 to 42" (95 to 105 cm) above the floor. The lower edge of the shade on floor lamps should be about 40 to 49" (100 to 123 cm) from the floor. Taller lamps used for reading should be positioned 15" (38 cm) to the side and 20" (50 cm) behind the center of the book when you're reading. Chandeliers should be suspended 34 to 36" (85 to 90 cm) above the surface of the table in dining areas, and well above a person's height in hallways and other walking areas.

The table lamp in the bedroom shown at right bathes the rest of the tabletop accessories in a cozy glow. You can use colored shades or specialty light bulbs to produce that type of warmth. Again, a lighting specialist can help you find the right shade and bulb to create the effect you want.

Back in the days when candles were extremely expensive, mirror-backed sconces and mirror-lined walls were used to reflect and multiply their precious light. It still works today. In the hallway shown above, light is bounced off and reflected by the mirrored sconce.

FOREST BY CANDLELIGHT

Since at least the eighteenth century, people have been decorating trees with lights, a Christian custom that probably stems from a much older pagan tradition of honoring the natural world and celebrating the warmth and comfort of light. In any season, for any reason, I love lighted trees.

You can use any sort of branches for this project, but we used sandblasted manzanita, which we found at a floral supply house. It's important to use common sense any time you combine dry wood with candles: Position the candle cups so the flames can't touch any of the branches. And, of course, never leave burning candles unattended.

1 Drill a hole in each mating branch. For each joint, glue a ½" (12 mm) piece of wire into the hole in one branch, then hot glue the mating branch in place. When the joints are dry, mold clay around each one to create a smooth transition.

2 Tape the branches into a large coffee can. Mix a batch of quick-setting cement, and fill the can. Set aside until the cement is dry.

3 Form balls of clay. Choose branches that will produce a balanced shape for the candelabra, and press the balls onto the tips of those branches. Mold the balls into candle cups, then scratch a texture onto the surface of the cups. Let the clay dry according to manufacturer's directions. Line the interiors of the cups with heavy-duty aluminum foil, then paint or stain the cups.

4 Set the coffee can inside an attractive pot and camouflage it with moss and stones.

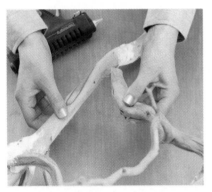
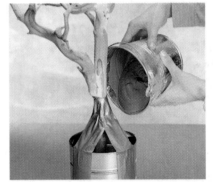

MATERIALS:

BARE BRANCHES • AIR-DRY CLAY • HOT GLUE • 12-GAUGE (2 MM) WIRE • LARGE COFFEE CAN
• TAPE • QUICK-SETTING CEMENT • HEAVY-DUTY ALUMINUM FOIL
• PAINT OR STAIN • PLANTING CONTAINER • SHEET MOSS

ALL THE TEA IN CHINA

My grandmother, master gardener and lover of dishes, got me started collecting teacups. I can still feel the pride with which I presented the latest prize from my travels and the way she beamed as she assured me that this was the prettiest one ever. Judging from flea market displays and antique store shelves, many others share our obsession.

1 *Drill a ½" (12 mm) hole in the center of each cup and saucer (see page 126). Stack the teacups and measure them. Purchase a threaded nipple that will accommodate the stack and leave about ½" (12 mm) at the top; purchase one 1" (2.5 cm) coupler for each inch of the nipple. (Allowing about 1" [2.5 cm] between cups, we used a 13" [33 cm] nipple and 13 couplers.) Slide a lock washer and a hex nut onto one end of the threaded nipple. Insert the nipple into the hole of the lamp base. Place a rubber washer over the nipple.*

2 *Set the first cup and saucer in place, add a rubber washer and a brass washer, then screw four brass couplers onto the threaded nipple. Add a brass washer and a rubber washer, the second cup, and a second set of washers; repeat to add the third cup. Screw on four more couplers, and top the assembly with a threaded brass washer, a harp, and another threaded brass washer.*

3 *Attach a socket cap to the nipple. Insert a lamp cord through the base and the nipple. Tie the split ends of the wire in an underwriter's knot, connect them to the lamp socket, and assemble the socket (see page 124). Add a lampshade and, if desired, a finial.*

MATERIALS:

CHINA CUPS AND SAUCERS (3 SETS) • THREADED NIPPLE
• LOCK WASHER (1) • HEX NUT (1) • 1" (2.5 CM) BRASS COUPLERS
(ONE FOR EACH INCH OF THREADED NIPPLE) • BRASS WASHERS (6)
• RUBBER WASHERS (6) • LAMP BASE • HARP • SOCKET CAP
• LAMP SOCKET • LAMPSHADE

IN THE MOOD

A candlelit garden is magical, and lighting a garden room with candles creates the same kind of magic. Hang candles from hooks or doorknobs or tree branches.

Spiral votive: Form a flat spiral at each end of a piece of 16-gauge (1.5 mm) galvanized wire. Use a dab of hot glue to hold the wire in place at each side of the votive holder. Cut a wire about 3" (7.5 cm) longer than the circumference of the votive holder. Form a small hook at one end and a flat spiral at the other. Wrap the wire around the votive holder and hook it in the front.

Beaded-mesh tea light: Cut a 1" (2.5 cm) strip of wire mesh to fit around a votive holder. At the front, lap the ends and weave a 3" (7.5 cm) piece of brass bead-ing wire through the mesh to join the layers. Bend the top of the wire down and string beads onto both ends; bend the ends up to secure the beads. Cut four 20" (50 cm) lengths of beading wire and fold each in half. At equal intervals, loop the beading wire around the wire mesh and twist, gathering the mesh. Use beads to join the wires in a diamond pattern, thread the wires through a brass bead, twist the wires together for about 2" (5 cm), then curl the ends.

Insulator Cap Votive: Form silver solder into a hanging loop; wrap 6 or 8 loops of 16-gauge (1.5 mm) wire around the top of an insulator cap, securing the loop. Add decorative accents, such as beads and tassels.

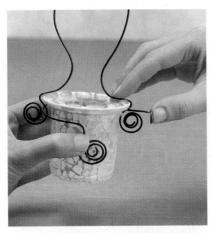

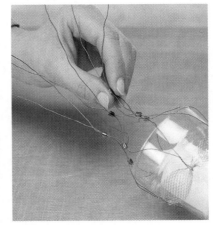

MATERIALS:

16-GAUGE (1.5 MM) GALVANIZED WIRE
• HOT GLUE • VOTIVE HOLDER
• VOTIVE CANDLE • WIRE MESH
• BRASS BEADING WIRE
• DECORATIVE BEADS • BRASS BEAD
• TEA LIGHT • INSULATOR CAP

BURNING BRIGHT

Originally designed to protect young plants during cold spells, cloches are beautiful as well as functional. Their graceful shape and handblown glass seem made to go with the glow of a candle. Throw in a little copper, and you've got a winning combination.

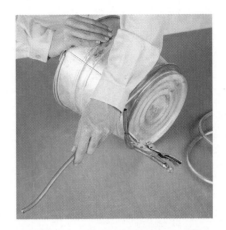

1 ▸ *Measure the circumference of the cloche to determine how big the hoops need to be. Flatten one end of a piece of flexible copper tubing, clamp it onto a garden pail, and shape it into a hoop. Mark and cut the tubing at the junction, then flare and solder the ends. Centerpunch three equidistant points on the hoop, then drill a ⅜" (9mm) hole at each point. Repeat to form two more identical hoops.*

2 ▸ *Cut three legs in a length appropriate for your cloche (ours are 15" [38 cm]). For each, flatten one end and clamp it to a 1" (2.5 cm) socket; hold the tubing firmly and ratchet the wrench to coil the tubing. At the second turn of the coil, bend the tubing at an angle to match the shape of the cloche. (If you don't have a socket set, wrap the tubing around a 1" [2.5 cm] dowel.) Cut nine 12" (30 cm) pieces of 12-gauge (2 mm) copper wire and wrap each around a piece of ¼" (6 mm) tubing to form nine 1"-long (2.5 cm) coils.*

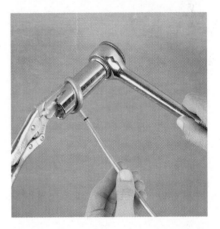

3 ▸ *Insert one leg into each hole in the first hoop; thread one of the wire coils onto each leg. Repeat with the second and third hoops. Clean and flux the joints; set the frame upside down and solder, working from the base of the frame up toward the legs. Before you solder the foot coils, adjust them to make sure the frame will sit level.*

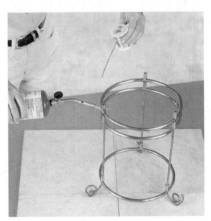

MATERIALS:

CLOCHE • ¼" (6 MM) FLEXIBLE COPPER TUBING
• GARDEN PAIL • 12-GAUGE (2 MM) COPPER WIRE

SHINING BRIGHT

This project relies on a new idea suggested by my bright and beautiful friend, Terrie Myers. Six-strand copper wire comes twisted—to create a hanging loop for this lantern, untwist and shape the wires. Ingenious—just like Terrie.

1 Cut an 18" (45 cm) piece of ½" (12 mm) flexible copper tubing and a 6-foot (1.8 m) piece of ½" (12 mm) rigid copper pipe. Form the flexible copper into a curlicue as shown; solder an end cap onto one end and a coupler onto the other. Solder the coupler to the copper pipe, using an elbow, to form a hook. Plant the completed hook in the soil of a large potted plant.

2 Untwist the first 10" (25 cm) of a 24" (60 cm) piece of twisted copper wire. Shape the individual strands around a round 6" (15 cm) chandelier globe; use one strand to band a pigtail at the bottom of the globe. Curl the tails around a dowel, then bend them into a pleasing arrangement. Wrap a piece of 16-gauge (1.5 mm) copper wire around the lip of the globe to cradle it within the wires. Form a loop at the opposite end of the twisted wire; untwist and shape the first 4 or 5" (10 or 13 cm) of each strand. Add sand and a votive candle, then hang the lantern from the hook.

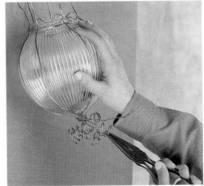

MATERIALS:
½" (12MM) FLEXIBLE COPPER TUBING • ½" (12 MM) COPPER PIPE
• ½" (12 MM) COPPER END CAP (1) • ½" (12 MM) COPPER COUPLER
• ½" (12 MM) COPPER ELBOW • 16-GAUGE (1.5 MM) COPPER WIRE • FINE SAND
• 6-STRAND TWISTED COPPER WIRE (2 FT. [60 CM]) • VOTIVE CANDLE • CHANDELIER GLOBE

$\mathcal{T}$ECHNIQUES

My dear friend Catherine once described her mother as a master at turning candlesticks into lamps and lamps into candlesticks. While this is probably not a skill you aspire to, we hope this book lights your creative fires and inspires you to make use of old materials in new ways.

As we were designing projects and deciding how to describe construction processes, our main goal was to make sure everyday people could actually do the things we suggested. As you look through these pages, we hope you'll think, "Hey! I can do that."

If a project uses materials or techniques that are new to you, you may need an introduction to some basic skills, whether it's wiring a lamp, soldering copper pipe, working with twigs, or drilling through ceramic or glass. Give yourself some extra time to get comfortable with the techniques and materials, and practice with scraps before you start working on a project. (Except for lamp wiring—that's a breeze.)

If you have questions after reading through the project and the background on the techniques required, you have a couple of options. First, most hardware stores or home centers have staff members who are happy to answer questions. Many home centers even have classes on the more involved techniques, such as soldering. When you buy materials, ask for help or additional information. If you're still having trouble, call or write to us. You can reach us at Creative Publishing international, 5900 Green Oak Drive, Minnetonka, MN 55343 or at DIY@creativepub.com. We love hearing from people who are bringing our ideas to life, and we especially love to see pictures of your creations.

Relax. Have fun. You really can do this.

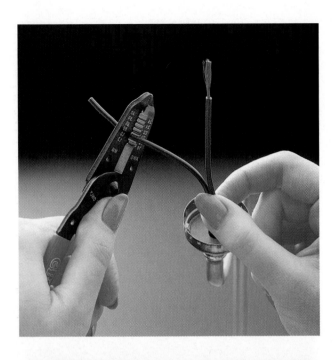

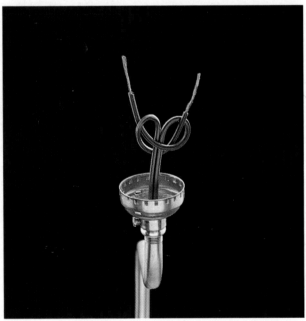

LAMP WIRING

The first time I made a lamp, I was surprised by how easy it was to do the wiring. I guess it seemed mysterious and complicated because I had no idea how few steps it really takes. Basically, all you have to do is thread the lamp cord through the base and up to the socket, and then connect two wires. Very simple—it will probably take less than half an hour to do the whole thing, even the first time. The next time, it will take just a matter of minutes.

Thread the lamp cord through the base and up through the lamp pipe and socket cap. (Many lamp cords are pre-split and the ends are stripped in preparation for wiring. If yours isn't, use a utility knife to split the first 2" [5 cm] of the end of the cord, along the midline of the insulation. Strip about ½ to ¾" [12 to 19 mm] of insulation from the ends of the wires.)

Tie an underwriter's knot by forming an overhand loop

with one wire and an underhand loop with the remaining wire; insert each wire end through the loop of the other wire.

Loosen the terminal screws on the socket. Look carefully at the insulation on the wires—the insulation on one wire will be rounded and on the other wire it will be ribbed or will have a fine line on it. Loop the wire on the rounded side around the socket's brass screw and tighten the screw. Loop the wire on the other side around the socket's silver screw and tighten the screw.

Adjust the underwriter's knot to fit within the base of the socket cap, then position the socket into the socket cap. Slide the insulating sleeve and outer shell over the socket so the terminal screws are fully covered and any slots are correctly aligned.

Test the lamp; when you're sure it works, press the socket assembly down into the socket cap until the socket locks into place.

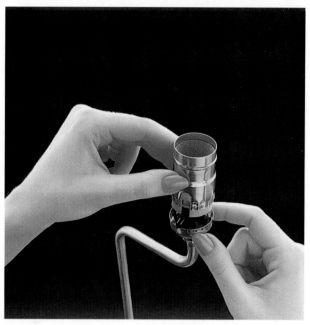

DRILLING HOLES IN CHINA

The first thing you need to do for a project like the teacup lamp is drill holes in the pieces. Many lighting stores and glass supply stores offer this service, but you certainly can do it yourself.

If you have a drill press and a hollow, circular diamond drill bit, use them. If not, you need a drill, a glass and tile bit, and some mineral spirits. If you need a large hole, start with a small bit; and gradually enlarge the hole by re-drilling with increasingly larger bits.

To drill a hole in a plate, put an X of masking tape on the front, at the center of the plate. Pour mineral spirits into the plate and begin drilling. Drill slowly and keep the bit perpendicular to the saucer. (The mineral spirits act as a lubricant and keep the saucer cool as the drill works its way through the ceramic.)

To drill a hole in a cup, pitcher, or jar, mark the center with masking tape, then put the piece upside down in a bucket of sand. Slowly drill the hole as described above—the sand will support the piece and make it easier to drill the hole without cracking or otherwise damaging it.

WORKING WITH COPPER

Soldering, or sweating, joints is much easier than you might imagine. If propane torches intimidate you, try one of the new, compact versions. The smaller size and quieter burn may feel more comfortable while you're learning. To solder a joint, use a propane torch to heat a copper or brass fitting until it's just hot enough to melt the solder. The heat then draws the solder into the gap between the fitting and the pipe, forming a strong seal.

As with many do-it-yourself tasks, you'll find that good preparation makes everything else much easier. To form a strong joint, the ends of the pipes and the insides of the the fittings must be clean and smooth. Soldering copper isn't difficult, but it requires some patience and skill. It's a good idea to practice on scrap pipe before taking on a large project.

The most common mistake beginners make is using too much heat. To avoid this problem, remember that the tip of the torch's inner flame produces the most heat. Direct the flame carefully—solder will flow in the direction the heat has traveled. Heat the pipe just until the flux sizzles; remove the flame and touch the solder to the pipe. The heated pipe will quickly melt the solder.

Plan to work on a heat-resistant surface or on a double layer of 26-gauge (0.5 mm) sheet metal. The sheet metal makes an effective shield, and its reflective quality helps the joints heat evenly.

If a series of pipe and fittings (a run) is involved, flux and dry-fit the entire run without soldering any of the joints. When you're sure the run is correctly assembled and everything fits, take it apart and prepare to solder the joints.

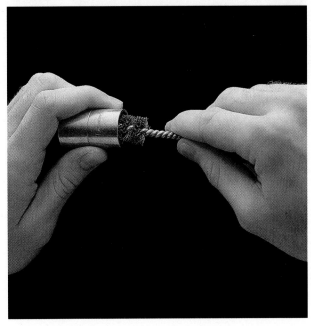

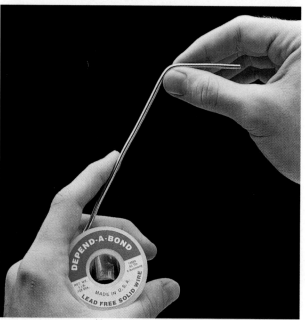

Sand the ends of the pipes with emery cloth and scour the insides of the fittings with a wire brush. Apply a thin layer of water-soluble paste flux to the end of each pipe, using a flux brush. The flux should cover about 1" (25 mm) of the end of the pipe. Insert the pipe into the fitting until the pipe is tight against the fitting socket. Twist the fitting slightly to spread the flux.

When you're ready to solder, unwind 8 to 10" (20 to 25 cm) of solder from the spool. To make it easier to maneuver the solder all the way around a joint, bend the first 2" (5 cm) of the solder to a 90° angle.

Light the torch and adjust the valve until the inner portion of the flame is 1 to 2" (25 to 50 mm) long. Hold the flame tip against the middle of the fitting for 4 to 5 seconds or until the flux begins to sizzle. Heat the other side of the joint, distributing the heat evenly. Move the flame around the joint in the direction the solder should flow. Touch the solder to the pipe, just below the fitting. If it melts, the joint is hot enough.

Quickly apply solder along both seams of the fitting, allowing capillary action to draw the liquefied solder into the fitting. When the joint is filled, solder will begin to form droplets on the bottom. A correctly soldered joint shows a thin bead of silver-colored solder around the lip of the fitting. It typically takes about ½" (12 mm) of solder to fill a joint in ½" (12 mm) pipe.

If the solder pools around the fitting rather than filling the joint as it cools, reheat the area until the solder liquefies and is drawn in slightly.

Note: Always turn off the torch immediately after you've finished soldering; make sure the gas valve is completely closed.

Let the joint sit undisturbed until the solder loses its shiny color—don't touch it before then—the copper will be quite hot.

When the joint is cool enough to touch, wipe away excess flux and solder, using a clean, dry rag. When the joint is cool, check for gaps around the edges. If it's not a good seal, take the joint apart and resolder it.

If you need to take apart a joint, reverse the process. First, heat the fitting until the solder becomes shiny and begins to melt. Then use channel-type pliers to separate the pipe from the fitting. Heat the ends of the pipe and carefully wipe away the melted solder. When the pipe is cool, polish the ends down to bare metal, using an emery cloth. Use new fittings when you resolder the joint.

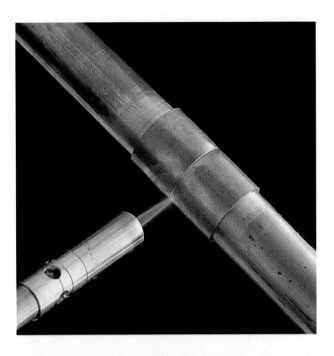

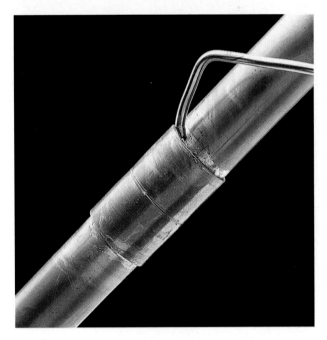

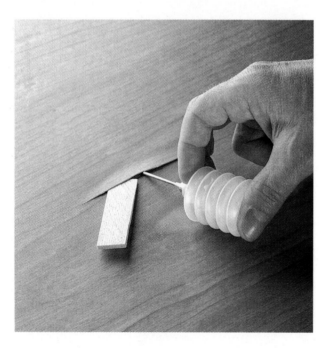

BASIC FURNITURE REPAIRS

Garden style often includes an eclectic mix of vintage and new pieces, and it's fun to shop for pieces that fit into the scheme of things. Signs of wear often are appealing, but some surfaces can and should be repaired.

Note: Original finishes add enormously to the value of a piece, and even aggressive cleaning can damage them. Certain types of repairs can drastically reduce the value of antiques. It's easy to alter an item and impossible to return it to its original condition, so think carefully before you act. Consult an expert if you have questions. If you bought the piece from a knowledgeable dealer, start there. If you have reason to believe the piece might be especially valuable, talk to an appraiser or a conservator.

The repairs we describe here are recommended for pieces that have appeal based on their style, color, and character rather than their value as antiques. If you want to refinish or restore an antique, do some research. Bookstores and libraries offer many fine books on the subject.

Veneer Repairs: Making basic repairs, such as re-gluing loose or blistered veneer, is a fairly simple job. Repairs involving patching should be left to professionals.

Before deciding to re-glue loose veneer, try using heat to renew the bond. Cover the loosened veneer with a damp cloth; press the cloth with a household iron set on low. Keep the iron moving—don't leave it in place for more than a few seconds. Wait for the veneer glue to liquefy, then remove the iron and the cloth. Before the glue rehardens, roll the area with a seam roller. Set a weight such as a heavy book on the area as it cools.

If ironing doesn't work, re-glue the loose spots. Use a putty or palette knife to lift the veneer so you can clean under it with a brush. Veneer is fragile—be careful not to tear it. If there's glue on the surface, scrub it with a cotton swab dipped in hot vinegar. Next, use a cotton swab or a glue injector to squeeze glue under the veneer. Cover the area with wax paper and a clamping block and clamp the area until the glue dries. Remove the clamp and carefully scrape away any excess glue with a chisel.

Missing sections of veneer are difficult to repair. If you still have the missing piece and it's intact, it can be re-glued in the way described above. If you don't have the pieces, get professional help. Cutting and gluing down new veneer patches is a job that requires finesse and experience.

Blistered veneer can be repaired in much the same way as loose veneer. Start by using a craft knife to slice the blister along the grain. Use a small brush to clean out any debris, then slip a thin spacer under the veneer. Inject carpenter's glue into the area, roll the blister with a seam roller, and cover the area with wax paper. Clamp or weight the loose veneer down until the glue dries. If the veneer overlaps at the seam, slice away the excess, using a craft knife and a straightedge.

Repairing Joints and Splits: Loose joints and split parts, common structural problems, usually can be corrected by gluing and reinforcing the joints.

Use wood sweller to tighten loose joints on parts that don't support much weight, such as interior spindles on a chair. Just squirt the wood sweller into the joint and let it sit—the wood in the joint will swell and tighten.

To repair a split spindle, start by cleaning debris and splinters from the pieces so the mating surfaces fit tightly. Apply glue to the mating surfaces, wrap the spindle with wax paper, then press the parts together. Slip hose clamps over the repair, spaced every 3 to 4" (7 to 10 cm); tighten the clamps. Let the glue dry, remove the clamps and paper, and scrape away the excess glue with a chisel.

Structural joints that need to support weight can be repaired with two-part epoxy. Drill at least two $\frac{3}{16}$"-diameter (5 mm) holes per joint. Using a self-mixing injector, deliver two-part epoxy glue into each hole. The epoxy will harden into "nails" that will reinforce the joints.

MAKING TWIG FURNITURE

If you like making something from practically nothing, you'll love building twig furniture. The only thing you'll need to buy is the nails, which makes it inexpensive as well as fun to do.

If you have wooded areas on your property, you can gather twigs and branches from your own trees. If not, contact builders in your areas to see if they'll let you gather wood on property that's scheduled to be cleared. Or, visit a brush recycling center. Tim's even been known to stop at commercial construction sites and ask for permission to scavenge through their brush piles. People sometimes laugh, but they rarely refuse.

Many kinds of wood will work for building twig furniture. Often the shape and diameter of the branches are more important than the variety of the tree. It's best to use freshly cut wood—it's easier to work with and as the wood dries, it shrinks around the nails, which makes for sturdier construction. As you scout for branches, consider the shapes you're trying to create and choose accordingly. Straight branches are often the best choices, but offshoots and curves will give your pieces dramatic flair.

The size of nails you should use depends on the diameter of the wood you're joining. If the nails are too large, they may split the twigs as they dry. Use 6d finish nails on branches 1" (25 mm) or more in diameter, 4d finish nails on twigs ¾ to 1" (19 to 25 cm) in diameter, and brads for twigs under ¾" (19 mm).

Before you start nailing branches together, drill pilot holes through the top branch and into the bottom one. Use a drill bit that's slightly smaller than the diameter of the nail, such as a ³⁄₃₂" (2.3 mm) bit for 6d nails and a ⁵⁄₆₄" (1.9 mm) bit for 4d nails.

If you're having trouble getting the pieces to stay in position while you drill or nail, try temporarily lashing them together with string or raffia.

After a piece of twig furniture has cured for at least a month, apply exterior wood sealer or a clear acrylic finish. Cover the entire surface of the wood, especially the cut ends of the branches.

CONVERTING PLANT CONTAINERS

Antique shops, flea markets, and garage sales are great places to find unusual or non-traditional containers that can hold plants. Any item in good condition can be made into a plant container if it can hold enough soil to support a plant and has adequate drainage.

Containers should also be durable enough to last for some time—being transplanted before it's had a chance to take root can traumatize a plant. Some containers are naturally tough, such as concrete chimney pots and troughs, old sink basins, and anything made of clay or galvanized metal. On the other hand, untreated wood eventually will rot if it's filled with soil and exposed to moisture.

Whimsical containers have a place in any garden setting, including garden-style rooms. Keep in mind, however, that using too many fanciful pieces reduces their impact. Try using just one or two special treasures in prominent places.

Before you decide to put a piece to use, assess its condition. Make sure any wood is free of rot and pests. You don't have to rule out clay, ceramic, or masonry pieces that have chips or minor cracks, but you should avoid pieces with major structural damage. Rust adds character to metal pieces, but edges that are rusted through may be dangerous or unstable.

A unique item doesn't have to become a plant container to earn a place in a garden-style room. If a piece isn't suitable to be used as a container, consider using it as sculpture, turning it into a furnishing piece, or adapting it to hold other plant containers.

To convert a piece into a plant container, start by soaking

it in clean water for several hours or overnight to loosen any debris. Using a mild detergent and a stiff brush, scrub the entire piece, particularly the surface of the planting area. Rinse the piece thoroughly, and then apply a disinfectant formulated to remove latent fungi or bacterial growth from planting containers. Thoroughly rinse the entire piece again, removing all residue, then let it dry.

Check the piece to see if it needs repair. Look for cracking, chipping, flaking, or other signs of damage that might affect the health of the plants in the container. If the piece is wood, prod all surfaces, especially the corners and the bottom, with a utility knife to evaluate it for rot. To protect wood from rot and pests, apply a horticultural preservative.

Porous pieces, such as unglazed clay and untreated wood, are especially susceptible to water damage from wet soil. With these materials, it's a good idea to waterproof the inside surfaces of the piece with a water-resistant compound (available from garden and hobby stores). Paint the inside surface of the piece with the compound; use overlapping horizontal strokes and make sure the entire surface is adequately covered.

With most pieces, the simplest way to create drainage is to drill three or four holes in the bottom. If the piece is clay or ceramic, you can prevent cracking or chipping by placing a piece of masking tape over the area before you begin drilling, and by using a carbide-tipped bit.

Cover each drainage hole with a section of thin zinc gauze or fine wire mesh. To filter out debris and provide additional drainage, add a layer of washed pea gravel to the container before you add the potting soil and plants.

AFTERWORD

More than in any other place I know, the spirit of gardening lives in a quiet glen beside a small creek in the middle of a suburban park. In a garden built by strangers and for strangers. This is its story.

On a beautiful spring day a few years ago, my friend Bryan and I went for a walk on a trail that circles a marshy area and some woods in a suburban nature preserve. My life was in chaos again. My teenage son and I were engaged in a power struggle from which no one could emerge a winner. He was dealing with the physical and emotional aftermath of a serious head injury suffered in a car accident. I was mourning the death of my image of myself as the great and powerful mother who could protect her children from all harm. Tough stuff.

As we walked, Bryan and I spied a small knot of crocus just beginning to bloom at the edge of the woods near the creek. They clearly had been planted there deliberately, though surely not by park personnel.

Touched clear through to my soul by the idea that someone had planted those bulbs for the pleasure of strangers, I visited them every day during their blooming. Their mere presence comforted me beyond words.

In the autumn of that year, we added a small patch of daffodils to the glen. It was a way to acknowledge, celebrate, and express our gratitude to the stranger who had planted the crocus that had brightened my mood earlier that year.

The next spring, we watched eagerly, and a little nervously, as the snows receded from the glen. The original crocus popped up, and to our surprise and delight, another small knot of crocus made an appearance. When those blooms faded, our daffodils took their turn. Shortly afterward, a small group of mixed bulbs joined the party, planted by unknown kindred spirits.

In the years since, we've added a few bulbs each fall and waited each spring to see what others have contributed. And now, from the earliest warmth of spring to the full blast of summer, there's always something blooming in this odd little garden. That first small act of kindness has given birth to a place of beauty that embodies the very spirit of gardening.

May that same spirit flourish in your home and your heart. Always.

jlf

INDEX

INDEX (CONT.)

PHOTOGRAPHERS

Mark Bolton
Garden Picture Library
London, United Kingdom
©Mark Bolton/garden picture.com: p. 54

Linda Burgess
Garden Picture Library
London, United Kingdom
©Linda Burgess/garden picture.com: p. 96

Crandall & Crandall
Dana Point, CA
©Crandall and Crandall: pp. 9, 33

Derek Fell's Horticultural Library
Pipersville, PA
©Derek Fell: pp. 10, 11, 17

Scott Francis
Esto Photographics
Mamaroneck, NY
©Scott Francis/Esto: p. 41

Gloria Gale
Overland Park, KS
Gloria Gale with the following photographers:
©Bill Mathews: pp. 8, 14, 23, 32, 42, 43, 44,
    65, 75, 97, 108, 110
©Ron Anderson: p. 57

Susan Gillmore
Esto Photographics
Mamaroneck, NY
©Susan Gillmore/Esto: p. 74

Saxon Holt Photography/PhotoBotanic.com
Novato, CA
©Saxon Holt: p. 64

Robert Kern
Fair Lawn, NJ
©Robert Kern for Kahn Struction: p. 24

A.I. Lord
Garden Picture Library
London, United Kingdom
©A.I. Lord/garden picture.com: p. 95

Karen Melvin
Architectural Stock Images, Inc.
Minneapolis, MN
©Karen Melvin: pp. 6, 25, 86, and for the
following designers: Carol Boyles Interiors p. 94;
Rob Gerloff Residential Architect, Minneapolis: p. 109;
Terry Gockman, Designer: p. 18;
Pam Powell Painting, St. Paul: p. 21;
Roddy Turner, Designer: p. 76

John Miller
Garden Picture Library
London, United Kingdom
©John Miller/garden picture.com: p. 56

Bradley Olman Photography
Redbank, N.J.
©Bradley Olman: pp. 12, 22, 85

Jerry Pavia Photography, Inc.
Bonners Ferry, ID
©Jerry Pavia: p. 45

Brad Simmons
Esto Photographics
Mamaroneck, NY
©Brad Simmons/Esto: p. 55

Janet Sorrel
Garden Picture Library
London, United Kingdom
©Janet Sorrel/garden picture.com: p. 107

Holly Stickley
Tigard, OR
©Holly Stickley: p. 16

CONTRIBUTORS

We would like to thank the following stores and companies for their generous support.

April Cornell
3565 Galleria
Edina, MN 55435
952-836-0830
www.aprilcornell.com

Apropylis
1520 East 46th Street
Minneapolis, MN 55407
612-827-1974
rajtarprod@worldnet.att.net

Crescent Moon
58 So. Hamline (@ Grand)
St. Paul, MN 55105
651-690-9630

Old World Antiques
4911 Excelsior Blvd.
St. Louis Park, MN 55416
952-929-1638

Smith & Hawken
3564 Galleria
Edina, MN 55435
952-285-1110
www.smithandhawken.com

Squire House Gardens
1129 Grand Avenue
St. Paul, MN 55105
651-665-0142

Photography contributors:

Bombay
1-800-829-7789
www.bombaycompany.com: pp. 15, 19B

Crate and Barrel
800-996-9960
www.crate and barrel.com: p. 19T

Pottery Barn
Williams-Sonoma Inc.
800-290-7373
www.williamssonoma.com: p. 87

Wood-Mode Cabinetry
800-635-7500
www.wood-mode.com: p. 4

CREDITS

President/CEO: Micheal Eleftheriou
Vice President/Retail Publishing: Linda Ball
Vice President/Retail Sales & Marketing:
Kevin Haas

Copyright © 2001
Creative Publishing international, Inc.
5900 Green Oak Drive
Minnetonka, MN 55343
1-800-328-3895
www.creativepub.com
All rights reserved.

Printed by Quebecor World
10 9 8 7 6 5 4 3 2 1

Library of Congress Cataloging-in-Publication Data

Garden style : ideas & projects for your world.
    p. cm. -- (Ideas with style)
    ISBN 1-58923-007-8 (pbk.)
    1. Interior decoration--United States--History--20th century.
2. Outdoor living spaces--Decoration--United States. 3. Decoration
and ornament--Plant forms--United States. 4. Garden ornaments and
furniture--United States. 5. Interior decoration accessories--United
States. I. Creative Publishing International. II. Series.
    NK2004 .G372 2001
    747--dc21
                            2001047250

Executive Editor: Bryan Trandem
Editorial Director: Jerri Farris
Creative Director: Tim Himsel
Managing Editor: Michelle Skudlarek

Authors: Jerri Farris, Tim Himsel
Editor: Barbara Harold
Project Manager: Tracy Stanley
Copy Editor: Tracy Stanley
Assisting Art Directors: Kari Johnston, Russ Kuepper
Mac Designer: Joe Fahey
Stock Photo Editors: Julie Caruso, Angie Hartwell
Technical Photo Stylist: Julie Caruso
Creative Photo Stylist: John Rajtar
Prop Stylist: Paul Gorton
Additional Project Design: Terrie Myers

Studio Services Manager: Marcia Chambers
Photographers: Tate Carlson, Andrea Rugg
Scene Shop Carpenters: Scott Ashfield, Dan Widerski
Director, Production Services: Kim Gerber
Illustrator: Jan-Willem Boer
Author Portraits by: Andrea Rugg
Cover Photograph by:
Karen Melvin for Roddy Turner, Designer

New from

CREATIVE PUBLISHING INTERNATIONAL

FLEA MARKET *Style*

Ideas & Projects for Your World

JERRI FARRIS AND TIM HIMSEL

Flea Market Style

This book features hundreds of ideas and dozens of projects for transforming flea market finds into reclaimed treasure. In some cases, it's simply a matter of finding the right setting for an object with an interesting shape, color, or texture. In others, a few inspired alterations create a whole new life in an entirely different role—an old panel door becomes a mirrored pland stand, for example. *Flea Market Style* gives readers complete instructions for creating dozens of simple but ingenious projects.

ISBN 1-58923-000-0 $19.95

CREATIVE PUBLISHING INTERNATIONAL

5900 GREEN OAK DRIVE
MINNETONKA, MN 55343

WWW.CREATIVEPUB.COM

PUYALLUP PUBLIC LIBRARY